The IOS Annual Volume 23: “Drought Will Drive You Even Toward Your Foe”

The IOS Annual

THE ISRAEL ORIENTAL STUDIES
ANNUAL DEDICATED TO THE ANCIENT NEAR EAST,
SEMITICS, AND ARABIC

Editor-in-Chief
Yoram Cohen

Section Editors
Amir Gilan (The Ancient Near East)
Nathan Wasserman (The Ancient Near East)
Letizia Cerqueglini (Semitic Languages and Linguistics)
Beata Sheyhatovitch (Arabic Language and Literature)

Scientific Board
The Ancient Near East
Yoram Cohen – Uri Gabbay – Amir Gilan – Maurizio Viano – Caroline Waerzeggers – Nathan Wasserman – Ran Zadok – Nele Ziegler

Semitic Languages and Linguistics
Werner Arnold – Alexander Borg – Letizia Cerqueglini – Christopher Ehret – Steven Fassberg – George Grigore – Benjamin Hary – Simon Hopkins – Frank Kammerzell – Geoffery Khan – Uri Mor – Matthew Morgenstern – Hezi Muzafi – Stephan Procházka – Aaron Rubin – Christian Stadel – Rainer M. Voigt

Arabic Language and Literature
Almog Kasher – Jeries Khoury – Giuliano Lancioni – Beata Sheyhatovitch – Kees Versteegh – Nadia Vidro

VOLUME 23

The titles published in this series are listed at *brill.com/iosa*

The IOS Annual Volume 23

"Drought Will Drive You Even Toward Your Foe"

Edited by

Yoram Cohen
Amir Gilan
Nathan Wasserman
Letizia Cerqueglini
Beata Sheyhatovitch

BRILL

LEIDEN | BOSTON

The Library of Congress Cataloging-in-Publication Data is available online at https://catalog.loc.gov
LC record available at https://lccn.loc.gov/2022050475

Typeface for the Latin, Greek, and Cyrillic scripts: "Brill". See and download: brill.com/brill-typeface.

ISSN 2772-784X
ISBN 978-90-04-52681-5 (hardback)
ISBN 978-90-04-52682-2 (e-book)

This book is printed on acid-free paper and produced in a sustainable manner.

Contents

Editorial VII

PART 1
The Ancient Near East

1 Urukagina's Rise to Power 3
Piotr Steinkeller

2 Samsuiluna and the Reconquest of Nippur 37
Nathan Steinmeyer

3 The Statue of Idrimi and the Term *mānaḫtu/mānaḫātu* 56
Yoram Cohen

4 On Aramaic Loanwords in Neo- and Late-Babylonian Texts: Morphophonological Classification, Documentary Distribution, General Evaluation, and Conclusions (Part Two) 66
Ran Zadok

PART 2
Semitic Languages and Linguistics

5 The Way to the Rainy Mountains: Semantic Networks of Natural Metaphors in Najdi Poetry 99
Letizia Cerqueglini

6 The Vocalization of Guttural Consonants in the *Secunda* and Other Hebrew Traditions 118
Isabella Maurizio

Editorial

Volume 23 of the Israel Oriental Studies Annual includes six articles. Four articles are found in the Ancient Near Eastern section. The first three deal with the history of Mesopotamia and ancient Syria: an investigation of the circumstances leading to Urukagina's rise to power based on his so-called "reforms," as well as on a variety of contemporary documentary evidence (Steinkeller); a reexamination of the reconquest of the city of Nippur by King Samsuiluna (Steinmayer); and a study of the term *mānaḫtu/mānaḫātu* appearing in the famous Statue of Idrimi (Cohen). The fourth article is the second and concluding part of "On Aramaic Loanwords in Neo- and Late Babylonian Texts" (Zadok). The first part appeared in IOS 21 (2021).

The Semitic section includes two articles. The first explores metaphors of rain and water in the Najdi poetry of the Bedouins of Arabia (Cerqueglini). The second article is concerned with the vocalization of guttural consonants of verbal forms in Origen's *Secunda* in comparison to other Hebrew traditions (Maurizio).

The title of volume 23, "Drought Will Drive You Even Toward Your Foe" (*al-maḥal yisūgak ʿāl-ʿadūwak*) is a Bedouin proverb (Cerqueglini, citing Clinton Bailey, *A Culture of Desert Survival: Bedouin Proverbs from Sinai and the Negev*. New Haven: Yale University [2004], p. 29) that encapsulates the difficult environment of a larger part of the Middle East. There is not a country in the region that has not felt the impact of climate change and difficult weather conditions in recent years, but all historians well recognize what a force water was throughout millennia in shaping the culture and history of the Middle East. In particular, water or lack of it were what was behind a form of livelihood so typical of this region from antiquity to the present—nomadism.

The IOS Annual is generously supported by the School of Jewish Studies and Archaeology, and the School of Cultural Studies, Tel Aviv University and by the Institute of Archaeology, The Hebrew University. The Editors thank managing editor Yael Leokumovich and acknowledge her contribution in editing this volume. We also extend our thanks to Isra Nashef, our Arabic editor.

The Editors welcome original studies in the languages, philology, histories and religions of the Middle East and the wider Mediterranean World. We invite scholars of the ancient Near East and related fields, such as Biblical Studies, the

Classics, and Archaeology of Mesopotamia, the Levant and the Mediterranean, scholars of Semitic and Afroasiatic languages and cultures, and scholars of Arabic, Arabic linguistics, socio-linguistics, dialectology, Arabic philology, philosophy, and literature to send in their contributions to the IOS Annual.

Information about in-house style and submitting a contribution can be found at http://www.brill.com/iosa.

Editor-in-Chief
Yoram Cohen

Section Editors
Amir Gilan and Nathan Wasserman, The Ancient Near East
Letizia Cerqueglini, Semitic Languages and Linguistics
Beata Sheyhatovitch, Arabic Language and Literature

PART 1

The Ancient Near East

CHAPTER 1

Urukagina's Rise to Power

Piotr Steinkeller
Harvard University
steinkel@fas.harvard.edu

Abstract

Urukagina of Lagaš is one of the best known figures of early Mesopotamia because his celebrated "Reforms," a document that, justifiably or not, is widely considered to be the first case of social reforms in the world. Past scholarship usually viewed Urukagina either as a usurper or a legitime ruler, who came to power because he was related to Lugalanda, his royal predecessor at Lagaš. This paper will attempt to throw additional light on Urukagina's rise to power, mainly by investigating three economic tablets from Urukagina's reign that have escaped detailed scrutiny until now, and also by re-evaluating Urukagina's "Reforms."

Keywords

Urukagina – reforms of Urukagina – Early Mesopotamia – Lagaš

תקציר

השליט אורכגינה (Urukagina) מן העיר לאגש (Lagaš) הוא אחת הדמויות המוכרות מראשית ההיסטוריה של מסופוטמיה וזאת בשל הצווים שלו (Reforms), הנחשבים כתעודה העתיקה בתבל אשר עוסקת בתיקון עוולות חברתיות. בעבר, חוקרים חשבו כי אורכגינה עלה לשלטון או כחומס שלטון, או כשליט לגיטימי, בשל היותו קרוב משפחה של לוגלנדה (Lugalanda), מי שהיה שליט של העיר לאגש. כוונת המאמר הנוכחי לשפוך אור נוסף על עלייתו של אורכגינה לשלטון. אנחנו נבחן שלוש תעודות כלכליות מזמן שלטונו של אורכגינה ונערוך דיון מחודש על אודות הצווים של אורכגינה.

מילות מפתח

אורכגינה – הצווים של אורכגינה – מסופוטמיה בתקופה הקדם-שושלתית – העיר לאגש

 | DOI:10.1163/9789004526822_002

المستخلص

اوروكجينا من لجش هو من أشهر الشّخصيّات في أوائل بلاد الرّافدين بسبب "إصلاحاته" المشهورة، وهي وثيقة يعتبرها الكثيرون، سواء بمبرّر أو لا، الحالة الأولى للإصلاحات الاجتماعيّة في العالم. كان الباحثون السّابقون ينظرون عادة إلى اوروكجينا إمّا على أنّه مغتصب للسّلطة أو أنّه حاكم شرعيّ، جاء إلى السّلطة لأنّه كان على صلة بلوغال أندا، ملك لجش السّابق. يحاول هذا المقال تسليط المزيد من الضّوء على صعود اوروكجينا إلى السّلطة، وذلك بشكل أساسيّ من خلال التّحقيق في ثلاثة أقراص اقتصاديّة من عهد اوروكجينا، والّتي لم تُدرس بالتّفصيل حتّى الآن، وأيضًا من خلال إعادة تقييم "إصلاحات" اوروكجينا.

الكلمات المفتاحيّة

اوروكجينا – إصلاحات اوروكجينا – بلاد الرّافدين القديمة – لجش

1 Introductory Remarks

Next to Gilgameš of Uruk and Sargon of Akkade, Urukagina of Lagaš may be the only figure of early Mesopotamia whose name is recognizable not only to scholars but also to the better-informed segments of the general public.[1] Urukagina owes this distinction due primarily to his celebrated "Reforms," a document that, justifiably or not, is widely considered to be the first case of social reforms on record.[2]

Another reason why Urukagina and his reign merit interest is the obscure circumstances of his rise to power. This problem was treated in the past by great many Assyriologists, who usually saw Urukagina either as a usurper or a legitime ruler, who came to power because he was related to Lugalanda, his royal predecessor at Lagaš. This paper will attempt to throw additional light

1 I am indebted to Marco Bonechi and Manuel Molina, who read the original text of this article and offered numerous suggestions for improvement, as well as to Andrew Pottorf for his expert editorial input. It goes without saying, however, that I alone am responsible for the final product. Text abbreviations can be found at BDTNS (http://bdts.filol.csic.es/index.php?p=principal_bibliografia) or CDLI (https://cdli.ox.ac.uk/wiki/abbreviations_for_assyriology).

2 A good illustration of Urukagina's popular appeal is the recent book by Max Everest-Phillips (2018), entitled *The Passionate Bureaucrat: Lessons for 21st Century from 4,500 Years of Public Service Reform*. Though written by a non-specialist, this book offers a remarkably exhaustive, accurate, and balanced overview of the evaluations of Urukagina's "Reforms" to date.

on this issue, mainly by investigating three economic tablets from Urukagina's reign that have escaped detailed scrutiny until now, and also by re-evaluating Urukagina's "Reforms."

Urukagina's reign was studied most recently by Ingo Schrakamp (2015). The great exhaustiveness of Schrakamp's article, which cites and discusses practically everything that was written on that subject until 2015, makes it unnecessary for me to reiterate that information. Therefore, when discussing specific points in the following discussion, I will simply refer to Schrakamp (2015).

2 The Transition from Lugalanda to Urukagina

The basic facts of Urukagina's accession are clear. He assumed power in the first month of Lugalanda's seventh year, meaning that the latter died either in that month or in the last month of the preceding year.[3] In either case, there was no gap between the two reigns. During his first regnal year, Urukagina held the title of ensik (henceforth Urukagina E 1). In his second year, he adopted the title of lugal, which he used subsequently (henceforth Urukagina L 1–10).

It is well established that Urukagina belonged to the Lagaš establishment prior to his rise to power.[4] There survive several attestations of him in sources dating to Lugalanda's reign. There, his name appears under the abbreviated form of Uru-ka. At that time, he bore the title of ugula-uku$_3$, the designation of a high military commander.[5]

Since extant sources make no mention of Lugalanda's sons, it appears certain that he died without male heirs. But Lugalanda had a brother, probably junior, who was named Ur-silasirsir.[6] This individual, who would have been Lugalanda's logical successor, died in year Urukagina L 1 at the latest.[7] He may still have been alive in the preceding year, i.e., Urukagina E 1.[8] But, even if Ur-silasisir was alive around Urukagina's succession, he probably would have been

3 Sallaberger and Schrakamp 2015, 72–73.

4 Schrakamp 2015, 310–311.

5 In all probability Urukagina's father was a certain Ur-Utu, who appears in the offering lists for the spirits of the former rulers of Lagaš and their relatives, which date to Urukagina's reign; Sallaberger and Schrakamp 2015, 72 and n. 168; Schrakamp 2015, 320–321, 371.

6 For Ur-silasirsir's attestations, see Balke 2017, 442–443. He is designated as a son of En-entarzi or simply as "son" (dumu).

7 He is one of the ancestors listed in Nikolski 1 25 iii 7 (year Urukagina L 1).

8 Zag-mu kiri$_6$ Gir$_2$-su^{ki}-kam Ur-sila-kam, "Zagmu, (belonging) to the orchard of Girsu (belonging) to Ur-sila⟨sirsir⟩" (DP 107 v 4–6, year Urukagina E 1).

quite old by that time. This could have been the reason why he was excluded from succession. Because of Ur-silasirsir's old age and possible frailty, it is possible that he had been judged unfit to become an ensik. If so, Ur-silasirsir would simply have been bypassed in favor of Urukagina.

There have been attempts to show that Urukagina was related by blood to Lugalanda's family, either by his own line or through his wife Sagsag. However, none of these speculations, whose intent was to demonstrate that his accession was "legitimate," has proved convincing.[9] One must assume, accordingly, that Urukagina was elevated to power through other means.

Here one needs to consider what royal "legitimacy" meant in Pre-Sargonic Babylonia. In addressing this question in the context of Urukagina's case specifically, scholars invariably assumed that one became a ruler at Lagaš through male descent or, in other words, that the kingship was hereditary. The history of the Lagaš kingship indeed shows a pattern of sons succeeding their fathers to the office of ensik. But this is only part of the story. In truth, the kingship of Lagaš was in principle elective, in that, at least as the official ideology had it, the ensik was selected from among the entire population of Lagaš by its titulary master and owner, the god Ningirsu.[10] This point is made explicit by Urukagina's "Reforms,"[11] which describe how Urukagina was chosen by Ningirsu from

---

9 See most recently, Schrakamp 2015, 332, 371, who speculated that Šubur-Bau, a brother of Barag-namtara (šeš munus), who is mentioned in Nikolski 1 199 i 6–ii 1 (year Lugalanda 4), was the same person as the son of Urukagina of that name. This would have made Lugalanda a son-in-law of Urukagina. However, in absence of any other data supporting this idea, a much simpler explanation is that these are two different men. Cf. Balke 2017: 389–390 and n. 1301. Schrakamp 2015, 334, 371, also suggested that Sagsag, Urukagina's wife was "*eine entfernte Angehörige der Herrsherfamilie*." But this idea too does not rest on any hard evidence. The only datum that could suggest a familial connection between Urukagina and Lugalanda is the fact that Urukagina's presumed son, A-en-ra-DU (Nikolski 1 219 ii 1–4: Sag_9-sag_9-ge A-en-ra-DU dumu e-na-ba; year Urukagina L 2), could be the same person as the "relative" (lu_2-su-a) of Lugalanda of that name, who is mentioned in VAS 25 19 ii 3 (Lugalanda year 3) and VAS 25 54 ii 3 (Lugalanda year 4). Cf. Schrakamp 2015, 328. One could then imagine that A-en-ra-DU had married into Lugalanda's family. But even this case is uncertain, since the sources dating to Urukagina's reign do not contain any other mentions of Urukagina's son called A-en-ra-DU.

10 Steinkeller 2017a, 119–120; id. 2017b, 13–14.

11 For reasons of convenience, in the following discussion I cite this source according to the edition by Frayne 2008. It needs to be noted, however, that this edition should be used only with the greatest caution. The "Reforms" are recorded in three inscriptions, which are: Ukg 1 = Frayne 2008, 248–265, Urukagina 1; Ukg 2 = Frayne 2008, 265–269, Urukagina 2; Ukg 3 = Frayne 2008, 269–275, Urukagina 3. Since Ukg 2 is essentially identical with Ukg 1, I generally refrain from citing it. Another, fragmentarily preserved text of the "Reforms," which records a different version of this document, was published by Vukosavović 2008.

among 36,000 Lagašites.[12] But ideology does matter, and so there must have existed a ritual procedure that enacted the process of divine selection. That procedure probably involved the performance of extispicies.[13] There also must have taken place an official confirmation and ordination of the new ensik, which, as one may expect, was carried out by the highest officials of the city-state, who, in this case, probably were the sanga officials, the heads of temple households. Further, it appears likely that this ritual procedure had a popular dimension as well. Even if common people were not part of the elective procedure *sensu stricto*, a public acclamation of the new ensik by them likely was required. This would mean that the population of Lagaš played at least some role, however minor, in the election of their rulers.

All of this was largely fictional, since under normal conditions the new ensik so "elected" would naturally have been either a son or a close relative of the former ruler. However, the case of Urukagina's "election" obviously was more complicated, since, as being unrelated to Lugalanda's family, he could not automatically have become an ensik. The only way for him to achieve that objective would have been through the securing of broad support for his candidacy, both from the high officialdom and the population of Lagaš at large. Because of this, it may *a priori* be assumed that Urukagina had made every effort to garner such forms of support. As I argue in the following, the sources extant offer ample evidence of Urukagina's efforts in that regard.

I begin with the evidence of VAS 27 33, DP 128, and DP 129.[14] These three related texts are records of the expenditures of barley and emmer to the "neighbors" (ušur$_3$) of the household(s) belonging to the gods Igalim and Šulšagana, sons of Ningirsu and Bau.[15] This economic organization, which is only rarely

12 Ukg 1 vii 26–viii 13. For a translation of this passage, which goes back to an earlier inscription of En-metena, see below p. 13. Other Sumerian rulers who claimed to have been selected by deities were En-metena, Gudea, and Ur-Namma. See below n. 34.

13 For the third millennium BC, only the selection of high priests through extispicies is documented. See, e.g., Ur-nimin dam ^{d}Nanše maš i$_3$-pad$_3$; Frayne 2008, 103–104, Ur-Nanše 17 iii 3–6. However, there is every reason to think that ensiks were selected in the same way. Here note that the ensiks of Lagaš are commonly said to have been "'found' by the heart" (šag$_4$-e pad$_3$-da) of Ningirsu and Nanše (Steible 1983, 272), where an extispicy almost certainly is meant. A related designation (Nibru^{ki}-a ^{d}En-lil$_2$-e pad$_3$-da) was later part of the titulary of Ur III kings. Cf. Frayne 2008, 222–223, En-metena 18 i 1″–8″, cited below in n. 34, where En-metena is said to have been granted by Enlil "a great scepter of destiny from Nippur." Very likely, this phrase too refers to an oracular selection.

14 For the transliterations of these three texts, see Appendix, Texts 1, 2 and 3.

15 The meaning of ušur$_3$/ušar$_3$ is "neighbor, person living the same city quarter"; cf. Schrakamp 2015, 312 and n. 69, who translates it "*Freund*"; cf. Selz 2014, 264 "*Nachbar*". Its Akkadian equivalent is *šēʾu, šīʾu*. See CAD Š/2 363; Steinkeller 1989, 242–243. Note the following

mentioned in the extant documentation, and thus remains elusive, was designated by the abstract term nam-dumu, best translated as "sonship."[16] In each instance, the occasion of the expenditures was the festival of Bau. In DP 128 and 129, practically the same group of recipients is recorded; many of them are also listed in VAS 27 33, which additionally names some other individuals.

VAS 27 33, which is the earliest of the three texts, concludes with a colophon reading (ix 1–x 1): "a total of 25 bushels of barley (and) 25 bushels of emmer; (these) are the emmer and barley allotments of the neighbors; Uruka(gina), the general, during the festival of Bau, allotted (this emmer and barley) to them".

The text is not dated, but, given the abbreviated writing of Urukagina's name and his title gal-uku$_3$, it must belong to the brief interregnum between Lugalanda's and Urukagina's reigns—either the last month of year Lugalanda 6 or the first month of year Urukagina E 1.

VAS 27 33 lists forty-eight individuals, receiving varying amounts of barley and emmer. The most common amounts are 18 liters of barley and 18 liters of emmer per person; the remaining (apparently higher ranking) individuals were allotted either 36 liters of barley and 36 liters of emmer or 72 liters of barley and 72 liters of emmer.

At least twenty-three of these persons are also listed in DP 128 and 129. For a discussion of the identities of all these individuals, see below.

---

attestations: 4 men ušar$_3$ da-gi$_4$-a-me, "neighbors in the city ward (among witnesses)"; MVN 3 330:10–14 = Steinkeller 1989, 241–242, no. 63; Ur III; galam-e ušur(LAGAB×SAR) kaš-de$_2$ ak-a[k], "a smart man makes a banquet for (his) neighbor"; Alster 1997, 208, 13.14; *išemmûma šīʾī bābija išabbusū*, "the neighbors in my city ward would hear about it and be furious"; "The Poor Man of Nippur," cited in CAD Š/2: 363b. NB: "friend" is not a synonym of "neighbor." While neighbors can occasionally be friends, the relationship between the two usually is adversarial. The standard Sumerian term for "friend" is ku/gu$_5$-li (Akk. *ibru*).

16 All the surviving data on the nam-dumu essentially date to Urukagina's reign. Our main source of information here are Urukagina's "Reforms," which identify it as the third most important—after the temple households of Ningirsu and Bau (e$_2$-mi$_2$, the House of the Woman)—economic establishment at Lagaš. Otherwise, information bearing on it is very scarce. The only source of significance here is Nikolski 1 18 (Urukagina L 1), which lists sixty-two employees of the temple-household of Igalim. In addition, there survive listings of the subordinates of Geme$_2$-^{d}Ba-u$_2$, Geme$_2$-sila-sir$_2$-sir$_2$, Šubur-^{d}Ba-u$_2$, and A-en-ra-mu-gi$_4$/A-en-ne$_2$-ki-ag$_2$, Urukagina's four children. For these sources, see Selz 1995, 62–63. These subordinates are described as lu$_2$ di$_4$-di$_4$-la-me, "the people of the Little Ones," where "the Little Ones" is an alternative designation of nam-dumu. It would appear, therefore, that the people in question were associated with the households of Igalim and Šulšagana. Organizationally, though, they appear to have been part of the household of Bau. See Maekawa 1973–1974, 120–131; Selz 1995, 53–55. The fact that these two households are poorly documented, and that the information on them is limited to the reign of Urukagina, probably indicates that, even though they had existed in some form earlier, it was only under Urukagina that they acquired the status of autonomous establishments.

What is remarkable about VAS 27 33 is that some of the names recorded in it are drastically abbreviated. See the following examples:

Ur-ka$_2$ (i 11) for Ur-ka$_2$-tur	Gan-Ba (v 5) for Gan-^{d}Ba-u$_2$
Me (ii 1) for Me-an-ne$_2$-si	Gu-ni (v 10) for Gu-ni-DU
Barag-a (ii 11) for Barag-an-ne$_2$	Ama-AB (v 13) for Ama-AB-e$_2$-ta
Geme$_2$-Ba (v 2) for Geme$_2$-^{d}Ba-u$_2$	Mu-a (vii 7, 8) for Mu-an-ne$_2$-dug$_3$

While abbreviations of personal names are common in the Pre-Sargonic sources from Lagaš, they are never that radical. This fact makes VAS 27 33 quite unique, suggesting that it was written in great haste, and that it may even have been composed by a scribe whose competence was somewhat lacking.[17] This suspicion is strengthened by the irregular composition of the text: while the standard Lagaš texts regularly place the commodity, the name of its recipient, and the recipient's patronymic/title in separate lines, in VAS 27 33 these are often combined in the same line, as in ii 1, 2, 3, 9, iii 9, iv 1, 3, etc. All in all, it appears as if this rushed record was occasioned by some sudden and unexpected event.

Passing now to DP 128 and 129, these two texts date to years Urukagina L 2 and Urukagina L 3 respectively. Thus, DP 128 is at least two years younger than VAS 27 33. In both texts, only emmer was distributed. The amounts per person were generally lower than in VAS 27 33—either 18 liters or 36 liters.[18] In either text, the colophon reads, following the total of the expended emmer: "(this is) the emmer allotment of the neighbors of the sonship (nam-dumu) of Sagsag, wife of Urukagina, king of Lagaš; for the festival of Bau, Eniggal, the manager, allotted it to them from the festival-house of Urukug."

DP 128 lists thirty-five recipients. The corresponding number in DP 129 is thirty-three. On the other hand, the latter source lists all the people appearing in DP 128, save for three individuals—Ar$_3$-tu ama ḪAR-sar-ra-ka (iii 7–8), Nin-e$_2$-⸢gissun-ni⸣ (iii 9), and Nin-šag$_4$-la$_2$-tuku (iv 7)—whose names it omits. On the other hand, it lists one additional person, who is Munus-sag$_6$-ga dam Lugal-ušur$_3$-ra sag-apin-ka (vi 6–8). The sequence of the recipients is the same in both texts,[19] indicating that DP 129 was composed based on DP 128.

17 Marzahn 1996, 11 suggests that this text is "*wohl* [*eine*] *Planungsunterlage*." But the complete absence of similar drafts among the surviving texts from Lagaš makes such a possibility unlikely.

18 The only exception is Ur-^{d}Ba-u$_2$ ašgab, who received 72 liters in both texts (DP 128 vii 2–3, 129 vi 4–5).

19 The only deviation is dam Za-u$_2$ šu-ku$_6$ (DP 128 iv 9–10), who is replaced by Za-u$_2$ šu-ku$_6$ in DP 129 vi 9–10.

As for the identities of the persons appearing in VAS 27 33, DP 128 and 129, they represent a wide range of professions and social strata. Most of them were women, either single or married. The husbands of the latter were a fisherman (šu-ku$_6$) and the head of a plowing team (sag-apin). It is possible that many, if not all, of these women were widows. Among them, one also finds a mother of a scribe (ama dub-sar), a doorkeeper (i$_3$-du$_8$), as well as three women who may be classified as "professionals": a midwife (nu-gig), a prostitute (geme$_2$-kar-ke$_3$), and an alewife (nig$_2$-DIN).[20]

As for the men appearing in these three texts, six of them were craftsmen. Those included two leather-workers (ašgab), a statue maker (taka$_4$-alam),[21] a stone-worker (zadim), a potter (bahar$_2$), and a carpenter (nagar). Among other men, there was a chief farmer (engar), a cook (muḫaldim), a roaster (gir$_4$-bil), a malt-maker (munu$_4$-mu$_2$), a gardener (nu-kiri$_6$), a vegetable grower (lu$_2$-sar), a bird chaser (dal-mušen), and a GAM.GAM (meaning uncertain, possibly "bent over, hunchback").[22] Finally, there were four men of higher-ranking status: a general (gal-uku$_3$), a brother of the sanga-GAR official,[23] a manager (nu-banda$_3$), and a foreman (ugula).

A great variety of professional designations, which range from the lowest ranking "bird chaser" to the high-ranking "general" is found in these three texts.[24] Note that is composition of people is typical of Babylonian neighbor-

20 For a discussion of this professional designation, see Steinkeller, forthcoming.

21 The term taka$_4$-alam designates both statues and their sculptors; Steinkeller 2017a, 91–92. Pre-Sargonic texts from Lagaš know also a lu$_2$-alam (e.g., VAS 14 16 ii 3), who probably took care of statues displayed in ritual environments, such as temples and the funerary chapels of deceased ancestors.

22 This designation appears also in several Ur III texts (e.g., AnOr 7 301 iii' 12), where it seems to describe elderly workers. I owe this information to Andrew Pottorf.

23 For this official, see below n. 39.

24 This evidence, especially the presence among the people in question of such low-status individuals as the prostitute, the alewife, and the bird-chaser, excludes any possibility of them having been "friends" of the royal family, as thought by Schrakamp 2015, 312 and n. 69. Lagaš sources mention yet another group of "neighbors," who were associated with the House of the Woman (e$_2$-mi$_2$). These individuals, who likewise were gifted foodstuffs by the royal family, are designated as either ušur$_3$ Barag-nam-tar-ra ... -me (DP 124 and DP 125; reign of Lugalanda) or ušur$_3$ e$_2$-mi$_2$-me (DP 126; Amherst 2; VAS 27 75; reign of Urukagina). Like the neighbors of nam-dumu, these individuals too show a wide range of professional designations. See also DP 161 i 3–ii 1 (Urukagina L [x]), which lists the expenditures of emmer for lu$_2$-su-a ensi$_2$-ke$_4$-ne, ušur$_3$ e$_2$-mi$_2$-ke$_4$-ne, and ušur$_3$ nam⟨-dumu⟩-k[e$_4$]-ne. The first of those, the lu$_2$-su-a, were relatives of Urukagina and his family. For this sense of lu$_2$-su-a, whose literal meaning is "the one of flesh," see the following data: [su-u$_2$] [SU] = *kim-tum, ni-šu-tum, sa-la-tum*; CAD K: 375; [SU] = *sa-la-tum*; RA 6 (1907) 132, AO 3930 rev. ii' 13'; su-za ga-an-ku$_4$, "may I enter your family! /

hoods.[25] Therefore, one needs to conclude that these ušur$_3$ nam-dumu indeed comprised a single group of people, who resided in the immediate area of the temple-household(s) of Igalim and Šulšagana.[26]

Of special interest here is the fact that these "neighbors" included three brothers of Urukagina's wife Sagsag. These individuals, who are listed only in VAS 27 33 ii 1–3, were Me-an-ne$_2$-si, Ur-^{d}Ba-u$_2$, and Igi-zi.[27] This suggests that Urukagina enjoyed a special connection with that neighborhood, perhaps even having been a resident of it himself.

Accordingly, the fact that these distributions of barley and emmer occurred precisely at the moment when Urukagina was positioning himself to become an ensik of Lagaš probably is not accidental. One could easily imagine that, by distributing these foodstuffs among his neighbors, Urukagina sought to gain their political support. In this connection one notes that, although Urukagina continued to gift the same individuals during the following years, it is striking that their number was later significantly lower and that the food so distributed

---

may I become your relative!"; "Gilgameš and Huwawa A", line 144; šagina šagina-mu-ne ama-mu [ni]n$_9$ šeš šeš-mu su-a [su-a-m]u-ne ki? ha-b[a-an-gar?]-re-eš, "(all) my generals, my mother, my sisters and brothers, (and all) my relatives I indeed settled? them (i.e., provided them with landed estates)"; "Ur-Namma Code", ll. 171–175. See also Selz 2014, 264. NB: The translation *"Bekannte"* of lu$_2$-su-a, offered by Schrakamp 2015, 312, n. 69 is to be corrected accordingly. The "relatives" of Urukagina appear also in VAS 14 106, which, importantly, lists Urukagina's sister (Gan-^{d}Ba-u$_2$ nin ensi$_2$-ka). In addition, there survive two records of the "relatives" of Barag-namtara (VAS 25 19 and 54). Five of the six individuals listed there—Geme$_2$-ub$_4$-kug-ga, Amar-ezem, A-en-ra-DU, Šubur-^{d}Ba-u$_2$, and Nin-e$_2$-MUŠ$_3$-še$_3$—are otherwise known as relatives of the royal family.

25 One finds a similar pattern of residence in the city of Umma in Ur III times. There too, in a neighborhood numbering 103 private houses, rich and poor lived beside each other, with their occupational backgrounds being equally diverse. See Nisaba 11 19 and YOS 4 300, discussed in Steinkeller, unpublished manuscript.

26 None of these individuals can be identified as members of the nam-dumu institution. The only exception is the female door-keeper Nam-šita-‹mu-bi-dug$_4$› (DP 128 v 8–9; DP 129 v 1–2), who possibly is the same person as her namesake, the doorkeeper of the e$_2$ ^{d}Igalim. See: 4(ban$_2$) Nam-šita 2(ban$_2$) dumu-munus i$_3$-du$_8$-am$_6$ (Nikolski 1 18 ix 6–8; year Urukagina L 1).

27 These three individuals appear in several sources dating to Urukagina's reign, where they are identified as šeš munus-me, "brothers of the Woman," where the "Woman" is Sagsag. See, in particular: land allotment ama munus (Sagsag's mother); land allotment Ur-^{d}Ba-u$_2$ ulu!-di!; land allotment Me-an-ne$_2$-si; land allotment Igi-zi; šeš munus-me (TSA 7 vii 6–15; year Urukagina L 4); land allotment ama munus; land allotment Ur-^{d}Ba-u$_2$; land allotment Igi-zi; šeš munus-me; … land allotment Ur-^{d}Ba-u$_2$; land allotment Igi-zi; šeš munus-me (DP 583 i 1–5, iii 1–3; year Urukagina L 2). For other attestations, see Balke 2017, 202–203, 284, 407.

consisted only of emmer. Also, the volumes of the expended grain were dramatically smaller: 792 liters in DP 128 and 780 liters in DP 129, against 3,600 liters in VAS 27 33. Should one assume, therefore, that, while it was still politically prudent to keep these people content, Urukagina no longer felt it necessary to be as generous as when he desperately tried to seize the throne of Lagaš?

In summary of this part of my discussion, I submit that VAS 27 33, DP 128, and DP 129 offer suggestive (if not conclusive) evidence of a propaganda campaign that Urukagina launched as part of his attempts to become a successor of Lugalanda. Behaving like a classic populist politician, Urukagina directed that campaign primarily at the less privileged of Lagaš. Further and even better evidence of these populist tactics is found in Urukagina's "Reforms," which is the subject of the section.

3 Urukagina's "Reforms"

Of course, Urukagina's "Reforms" is a misnomer: there does not exist such a document. What we have instead is a list, imbedded in three of Urukagina's building inscriptions, of the various abuses that he allegedly redressed following his ascent to the throne of Lagaš. Since building inscriptions were addressed to the divine audience,[28] and not to the earthly one, Urukagina's message, at least in this written version, was not accessible to the population of Lagaš at large. There are strong reasons to think that this message was disseminated publicly, though we will never know how it was done and what exact form it took.[29] This, in my view, can be inferred from the strong populistic tenor of the version we have, and from some of the peculiarities of the text. Here of special significance are the sections specifying the reductions of funerary, divorce, and marriage fees that Urukagina allegedly instituted.[30] These sections are too detailed and specific to be but an empty claim. Whether or not Urukagina did deliver on his promises, these reductions undoubtedly had been announced officially, and so there must have been a way in which this was communicated to the general population.

---

28 Steinkeller 2017a, 11.

29 One of the means of such dissemination may have been town-criers (nimgir), who are known to have publicly announced the conclusion of legal transactions, such as the sales of houses and orchards; Steinkeller 1989, 101–102. Very likely, these officials were also responsible for the publicizing of royal enactments and city ordinances.

30 Ukg 1 vi 4–27, Ukg 3 ii 15′–31′.

I further submit that the populistic tenor of the text at our disposal indicates that the actual reforms were promulgated just before Urukagina's succession, during the short period when he was trying to sway public opinion in his favor—or "to win the hearts and minds" of Lagaš, so to speak. If so, these reforms—or promises, more correctly—formed a crucial element of his electoral strategy. On the other hand, the written "Reforms" must date to year Urukagina's year L 1 or slightly later. This is demonstrated by the fact that, in that text, Urukagina is already described as a lugal, "king," of Lagaš.[31]

The text of the "Reforms" consists of two sections, recording the former abuses and Urukagina's redresses respectively. The two are connected by the following passage (Ukg 1 vii 26–viii 13):

> Such indeed was the rulership ($\text{pi-lu}_5\text{-da}$)[32] of the former days (referring to the abuses listed earlier). When Ningirsu, warrior of Enlil, granted the kinship (nam-lugal) of Lagaš to Urukagina, selecting him from among 36,000 people, he (Urukagina) restored the destinies of the past.[33] He seized the words/commands that his master Ningirsu had spoken to him.[34]

The text then lists the changes instituted by Urukagina, concluding with the words "thus he had spoken" ($\text{i}_3\text{-dug}_4$; Ukg 1 xii 12), where the subject is apparently Ningirsu rather than Urukagina.

Appended to the text is an additional section (Ukg 1 xii 13–28), which describes how Urukagina amnestied various kinds of felons and criminals,

---

31 For the significance of this political move, see below p. 19.

32 The term $\text{pi-lu}_5\text{-da}$ is a loanword from the Akkadian *bēlutū*, "rulership, dominion, royal authority." In its Pre-Sargonic usage, it undoubtedly had a pejorative sense, signifying an authoritative royal rule, such as existed at that time in northern Babylonia, and whose primary example was the kingship of Kiš; Steinkeller 1987, 58. Therefore, by using this term Urukagina means that the former ensiks of Lagaš practiced that oppressive form of rule and domination.

33 Here the determinations of destinies, which were yearly carried out by the collegium of the chief deities, are meant. See in detail Steinkeller 2017b, 12–17.

34 This passage echoes an earlier inscription of En-metena: [...] ⸢xx⸣ [šag_4 l]u_2 36,000! [šu]-ni ba-ta-[dab_5]-ba-a [gidri] mah nam-ta-ra $^{\text{d}}\text{En-lil}_2$-le Nibru^{ki}-ta En-TE.ME-na-ra mu-n[a]-a[n]-sum, "(when Ningirsu ...) selected (En-metena) from among 36,000 people, Enlil granted to En-metena a great scepter of destiny from Nippur"; Frayne 2008, 222–223, En-metena 18 i 1″–8″. Nearly three hundred years later, Gudea of Lagaš described his selection by Ningirsu in similar terms. See "Gudea Statue B" iii 6–11, viii 11–18, discussed by Steinkeller 2017b, 13 and n. 46. As suggested by Steinkeller 2017a, 33, n. 49, Gudea's account draws directly on the inscriptions of Urukagina and En-metena in

establishing their freedom (ama-gi$_4$).[35] This section concludes with the statement: "that (in the future) the widow and the orphan are not subjected to the powerful one, Urukagina made a covenant with Ningirsu (inim-bi inim e-da-keš$_2$)."[36] One may assume that the "covenant" in question extended to Urukagina's redresses as well.

The main questions raised by the "Reforms" are who were the respective perpetrators and victims of the abuses and who were the beneficiaries of the redresses?

The main culprits clearly were the (former) governor and his immediate family, who are accused of having used the resources of the temple households of Ningirsu, Bau and their two sons for their own benefit. Specifically, the "Reforms" accuse them of turning the best lands of temple households into their own garlic and cucumber fields, and of using the plowing teams of those institutions for that purpose (Ukg 1 iv 9–18, Ukg 3 i 22′–26′). In this way, they deprived the heads of temple households of the use of their own donkeys and oxen (Ukg 1 iv 19–22).[37] As a result, the ensik's family had accumulated so much agricultural land and buildings that those properties virtually crowded one another (Ukg 1 vii 5–11).

Other abusers were various subordinates of the ensik, among them, the official in charge of boats and sailors, the chief shepherds of donkeys and sheep, and the inspector of fisheries (enkud), who used their offices to enrich themselves and took advantage of their underlings (Ukg 1 iii 5–13).[38]

---

question. Another ruler who claimed to have been divinely selected was Ur-Namma: bala Ur-^{d}Namma lugal nig$_2$-si-sa$_2$(A) ^{d}Namma uku$_3$-e ba-il$_2$-la-ta, "since the reign of Ur-Namma, king of justice, who was elevated by Namma from among the people."; "Ur-Namma Laws", CUSAS 17 107, x ix 18–19.

35 For this passage, see Steinkeller 1991, 227–229, 232.

36 The literal sense of this idiom is "to bind a word with a word."

37 These lines are a logical continuation of the preceding passage, and thus the sanga officials were the victims and not the abusers (as the translators of these lines usually assume): anše sur$_x$(EREN$_2$)-ra gud du$_7$-du$_7$ sanga-sanga-ne e-ne-keš$_2$-ra$_2$-am, "(the use) of the donkeys of (plowing) teams (and) of the finest oxen was restricted/denied to the heads of temple households." Note that the following lines (Ukg 1 v 1–3) describe how the barley of the sangas was appropriated by the ensik's personnel. I assume that keš(edr), "to tie," is used here in the sense of "to restrict, to deprive." Cf. id$_2$-Idigna gu$_2$ min-a-ba bi$_2$-in-dab$_5$ sig-še$_3$ Ki-en-gi-ra$_2$ gana$_2$ bi$_2$-in-keš$_2$ igi-nim-še$_3$ gir$_3$ i$_2$-keš$_2$, "(Tirigan) seized both banks of the Tigris; in the south, in Sumer, he blocked (water) from the fields, in the north, he closed off the roads"; Frayne 1993, 283–293, Utu-hegal 4:39–43.

38 In Ukg 1 iii 11, the mysterious $^{u3-mu2-u2}$umu$_x$(KA×SAR) must describe fish in some way, since it parallels the earlier-mentioned boats, donkeys, and sheep. For the abuses of the inspector of fisheries, see further Ukg 3 ii 10′–14′: dumu ukur$_3$-ra$_2$-ke$_4$ ḫur SAG×ḪA-na u$_3$-mu-ak ku$_6$-bi lu$_2$ ba-dab$_4$-kar-re$_2$ lu$_2$-bi i$_3$-^{d}Utu i$_3$-e, "when the son of a pauper

The sanga-GAR, whose exact role is uncertain,[39] but who must have worked for the ensik as well, is said to have unlawfully cut down trees in the garden of a "pauper's mother" (ama $ukur_3$-ra_2) and bundled off their fruits (Ukg 1 v 22–vi 3). Also implicated were the employees of the ensik's private household ($eren_2$ $ensi_2$), who are said to have divided among themselves the barley of the heads of temple-households (še sanga-sanga-ne e-ba) (Ukg 1 v 1–3).

The ensik was also blamed for the imposition of excessive taxes and fees. Note the following:

(1) The purification priests ($guda_4$) were required to make barley deliveries (a portion of their income?) to Ambar (one of the main agricultural areas of the Lagaš city-state) and even to build grain silos there for those deliveries (Ukg 1 iii 14–17, Ukg 3 i 5′–9′).

(2) The shepherds had to pay a penalty if their wooly sheep died of heat stress (Ukg 1 iii 18–iv 1).[40]

(3) Another penalty was levied on the lambs owed to the ensik by field-measurers, chief gala priests, stewards, brewers, and foremen (Ukg 1 iv 2–8).[41]

---

made a fishpond for himself, one was taking away (his) fish, that man kept on crying out: 'O Utu!'". The syntagm ḫur SAG×ḪA-na probably is ḫur $ḫu_x$-ani-ak, "hole of his fish," where $ḫu_x$(SAG×ḪA) stands for ku_6. Cf. Civil 1983, 565–566.

39 As shown by the writing sanga-GAR-ke_4 in Ukg 1 v 22, this title is a genitival construction. However, the reading of GAR is unclear. If it is ninda, "food," sanga-GAR might have been an official in charge of food stores. This functionary is common in Fara texts; Visicato 1997, 126. However, as far as I know, the Fara texts do not mention any other types of sangas (except those named in the colophons of lexical and literary texts). It is possible that sanga-GAR was an ancient title, which survived only in Pre-Sargonic Lagaš and Umma (later sources do not mention it). At Lagaš, the sanga-GAR belonged to the highest stratum of the society. Note that the wife of a sanga-GAR was a relative of Urukagina's family (VAS 14 106 ii 5–7). She also counted among the select group of ladies, receiving ritual allotments of holy milk and malt (DP 133×9, year Urukagina L 1; TSA 5 rev. ii 12, year Urukagina L 2). Several sources dating to Lugalanda's reign mention a sanga-GAR named Ur_2-mud (DP 42 ii 8–9; 59 vi 18–19; 399 i 3–4). The Umma attestations of sanga-GAR do not throw light on his role; e.g., CUSAS 14 147, 158, 170, 258; CUSAS 33 126 rev. 3, 43 iii 2. The only exception may be CUSAS 35 397 i: 240 ninda / PN / sanga-GAR / e_2-gal / de_6, "240 breads, PN, the sanga-GAR, delivered to the "palace,"" which could point to his involvement in the storage and distribution of food.

40 See in detail the excursus, pp. 28–33.

41 Specifically, the penalty was for the lambs which were qualified as gaba. The most likely meaning of gaba is "weaned"; Steinkeller 1995, 54–55. However, it is difficult to see why such a normal condition of lambs should call for a penalty. Most likely, therefore, gaba, "breast," describes some medical problem affecting lambs. According to Ukg. 3 i 11′–21′, the same professionals were required to shear their wooly sheep in the "palace." And if their sheep died of heat stress, their wool was confiscated by the "palace," and in addition they had to pay a penalty of 5 shekels of silver per sheep. For this passage, see the excursus.

(4) The heads of temple households (sanga) were required to deliver to the ensik's "palace," in lieu of their corvée obligation (dubšig(IL_2)-$še_3$ i_3-il_2-am_6), various textiles, linens, leather and metal objects, spices, and other, difficult to identify items (Ukg 1 v 4–21).[42]

(5) The population of Lagaš had to pay a wide range of funerary fees; although those were collected by various funerary personnel, their ultimate beneficiary undoubtedly was the ensik himself (Ukg 1 vi 4–27).

(6) There were also fees for the authorization of divorces and marriages.[43] The divorce fees were paid to the ensik and the grand vizier (sukkalmah), and the marriage fees to the ensik, the grand vizier, and the $abgal_2$ priest (Ukg 3 ii 15′–31′).[44]

(7) The craftsmen were forced to deliver (to the ensik's "palace") freight wagons (Ukg 1 vi 28–vii 1).[45]

(8) Laborers, possibly when returning to the city from work assignments, had to pay a toll at the city gate (Ukg 1 vii 2–4).[46]

A key element of this exploitative system were the ensik's bailiffs (maškim), who operated throughout the city-state, executing, apparently, the collection of unpaid taxes and fees, and dragging the offenders to court (Ukg 1 vii 12–16).[47]

---

42 The "palace" is mentioned specifically in the corresponding redress (Ukg 1 ix 2–6). For the question of the royal "palace" in Pre-Sargonic Lagaš, see Steinkeller 2019, 127–130.

43 lu_2 sag šimbi i_3-ni-de_2, "when one poured aromatics over the (bride's) head" (Ukg 3 ii 22′).

44 For this official, see Steinkeller 2017a, 65–73, 76, 86.

45 giš-kin-ti nig_2-šu il_2-la i_3-tuku, "the craftsmen had (an obligation) to deliver freight wagons." For nig_2-šu(-ak), a type of freight wagon, see Civil 2008, 108. See also Nikolski 1 14, which lists twenty-six men who were conscripted for these contraptions (nig_2-šu-$še_3$ ba-lah_4-$eš_2$), apparently, to pull them.

46 For this passage, see Steinkeller 1978, 74. Laborers = guruš-min-me (Ukg 1 vii 2). Note the writing guruš-min-ma-ka /guruš-min/m-ak-a(k)/ in Vukosavović 2008, 6–7; CUSAS 11 352 iii′ 7′ = CDLI P235683, a variant ms of Ukg 1. That guruš-min is a genitival construction is confirmed by the following passage: 2(gur) mun ⌜gur⌝ guruš-min-ke_4 šu ba-ti; TCBI 1 184:1–3; Sargonic. The term guruš-min, "double workers," mentioned there apparently designates the main worker and his substitute. In other Pre-Sargonic sources from Lagaš, such pairs of workers are designated as sag-dub, "the main worker (lit.: the one listed at the top of the tablet)" and šeš-sur_x($EREN_2$)-ra, "the 'brother' of the team." See Maeda 1982, 70 and 81; id. 1983, 67. In Ur III and Old Babylonian times, substitute workers were called dirig or *(w)atru*, "extra, supernumerary"; CAD A/2: 500.

47 In Ukg 1 vii 15, the bailiff is called maškim di, where di means either "the one on the move, acting" (grammatically: di-e), or "(the one of) legal cases." This designation is missing in the corresponding redress: maškim nu-e, "the maškim was not acting" (Ukg 1 ix 22–25).

Among the victims of the abuses were the heads of temple households, who, as we have seen earlier, were heavily taxed by the "palace," and whose plowing teams and stores of barley were used by the ensik's private organization. Another victim were the purification priests ($gudu_4$), whose barley supplies were also taxed by the ensik.

The main victim of the alleged abuses, however, was the entire population of Lagaš. But, although the wronged parties included some of the higher-ranking individuals,[48] the primary concern of the "Reforms" clearly was the less-privileged ones, the ordinary citizens who were prosperous enough to own their orchards, fishponds, sheep, and donkeys. This concern extended even to dependent laborers such as the blinded workers (igi-nu-du_8) employed in orchards (Ukg 1 vii 17–25).

More fundamentally, the "Reforms" are about social justice in its ideal form, that the richer and more powerful one does not exploit those who are less privileged than he. In this way, the RU-lugal people, who were part of the ensik's private organization,[49] could simultaneously count both as the oppressors and the oppressed: in the first case, when they illegally seized blind individuals, forcing them to work in their gardens (Ukg 1 vii 17–25, Ukg 3 ii 1′–9′); and in the second case, when they were compelled by their foremen (ugula) and the "big men" (lu_2-gu-la) to sell them their donkeys and houses at lower prices (Ukg 1 xi 20–31, Ukg 3 i 2′–4′).

The redresses of all these abuses, as described in the "Reforms," constituted reversals of the former situations. There is no need, therefore, to describe them in detail.

For the purposes of the main topic of this paper, which is the question of Urukagina's rise to power, the main points of importance about the "Reforms" are, first, the fact that this document puts blame for the alleged abuses squarely on the (former) ensik and his family. Second, it identifies the victims of the abuses as: (1) the deities of Lagaš; (2) the heads of temple households (who acted as the earthly representatives of those deities and whose interests they guarded); and (3) the population of Lagaš at large.

Although the ensik referred to in the "Reforms" is never named, Lugalanda obviously is meant here. That Urukagina had been able to make such an accusation at all, however indirect it was, was possible *only* because he was not related to Lugalanda and his family. Otherwise, such an accusation would have been unthinkable.[50]

48 Like the ones mentioned above p. 15, under (3).

49 For this category of people, see below n. 62.

50 This fact alone excludes any possibility of him being related to Lugalanda's family.

In summary, the "Reforms" emerge as a propaganda tool, which was one of the means Urukagina employed to become an ensik of Lagaš.[51]

As for the "Reforms" veracity, there are no textual data that would allow us to verify if any of the redresses Urukagina claimed to have instituted were ever implemented in real life.[52] However, certain developments of his reign make one feel rather skeptical about such a possibility.

4 How Urukagina Consolidated His Rule Over Lagaš

The surviving members of Lugalanda's clan—if such existed—may understandably have resented Urukagina's succession. Urukagina himself did his best not to display any animosity toward them, at least overtly. In fact, he took every opportunity to show that he was Lugalanda's rightful successor and that he venerated his memory. The best illustration of this is the fact that, throughout his reign, Urukagina dutifully presented offerings to the spirits of Lugalanda and his deceased kin, among them, his wife Barag-namtara, his father En-entarzi, his grandfather Dudu, and his aforementioned brother Ur-silasirsir.[53] He also paid all due respects to MesanDU, who was the personal god of Lugalanda's family.[54]

Urukagina's efforts to present himself as a legitimate Lagašite ruler reached even deeper into history past. Thus, although his personal god was Ninšubur, on occasion he claimed that the deity in question actually was Šul-PA×MUŠ, the personal god of the family that ruled over Lagaš before En-entarzi and his successors, beginning with Ur-Nanše and ending with En-anatum II.[55] Clearly, by appropriating Šul-PA′MUŠ, Urukagina intimated that he descended from Ur-Nanše's family, and, therefore, that his rights to the office of the ensik of Lagaš superseded those of Lugalanda.[56]

51 While accentuating this point, my evaluation of the socio-economic and historical significance of the "Reforms" is in many respects similar to those offered by Schrakamp 2015, 340 and Selz 1999–2000, 15–20 (discussed by Schrakamp 2015, 339–340).

52 However, see the ambiguous case discussed below in the excursus.

53 DP 57; Nikolski 1 25; TSA 9; VAS 14 137; VAS 14 164; VAS 14 172; VAS 27 85; etc.

54 See Steinkeller 2019, 125 and n. 37.

55 Ninšubur: Frayne 2008, 279–280, Urukagina 6 iv 10–v 1; ibid., 282–283, Urukagina 8 v 6–7; Šul-PA′MUŠ: ibid., 283, Urukagina 9:12′–13′.

56 There are reasons to suspect that En-entarzi, father of Lugalanda, became an ensik by overthrowing the heirs of En-anatum II, his immediate predecessor. See Steinkeller 2019, 126–127.

Whatever difficulties Urukagina may have faced while striving to become an ensik of Lagaš, it is clear that, already in the second year of his reign (year Urukagina L 1), he was in full control of that office. This is made certain by the fact that, in that year, he assumed the title of lugal of Lagaš.[57] This move clearly reflected his growing political ambitions, for this title meant a stronger, more authoritarian form of kingship.[58]

Needless to say, by becoming a lugal Urukagina did exactly the opposite of what he had promised in his "Reforms": rather than rejecting the concept of the authoritarian monarchic rule—the pi-lu$_5$-da of the former days—he made it even stronger and more pervasive. This development also represented a radical departure from the past tradition. Although this title had been used by Ur-Nanše, the first ruler of Lagaš of whom extensive information survives, all his successors had to be content with the more modest title of ensik, probably in recognition of the enduring strength of the notion that the society formed an egalitarian temple-community, which shared all the resources equally, and whose embodiment was the institution of temple households. Given that the temple households controlled most of the resources of the city-state, the secular ensiks, who represented a relatively recent development, were locked in the constant struggle with the heads of temple households for the political rule over the city-state.[59]

That ideal temple-community, with its ancient norms and values, is in fact what Urukagina had promised to restore to Lagaš in his efforts to become its ensik. But that temple-community, as it appears to have existed in the Late Uruk period, possibly surviving into ED II times, had long since been but a dream, a memory of paradise lost. Due to internal developments, and the example of the political organization of northern Babylonia, which was characterized by the existence of strong hereditary kingship, at Lagaš too tendencies toward a more authoritarian rule, a more economically stratified society, and

57 Interestingly, in one of the inscriptions recording the "Reforms," Urukagina is said to have been selected by Ningirsu as a lugal of Girsu (Ukg 2 i 3–5, ix 1′–2′; probably also in iv 4–5, reconstructed). He is assigned this title also in two other sources (Frayne 2008, 275–279, Urukagina 4 viii 8–9; and 286, Urukagina 13:4). The reason behind these alternative titles is unclear. It appears that Urukagina used them simultaneously, since Frayne 2008, 275–279, Urukagina 4, an inscription describing the sack of Lagaš by Lugal-zagesi, must date to the later part of his reign. The title of lugal Girsu may have been less ambitious. Be that as it may, this varied titulary could indicate a degree of uncertainty on behalf of Urukagina about his political status.

58 For the significance of this title, especially as it was used by the Pre-Sargonic rulers of Kiš, see Steinkeller 1993, 120; id. 1999, 112; id. 2013, 146. Cf. Schrakamp 2015, 342–347.

59 Steinkeller 2019, 122–132.

the private ownership of agricultural land had taken root. By Urukagina's time, those tendencies had become so strong that, even if his intentions of bringing the "traditional values" back to Lagaš were sincere, that goal would have been unreachable.[60]

In this connection, yet another factor needs to be considered, and that is the international situation at Urukagina's succession. At that time, all the neighbors of Lagaš had strong and aggressive rulers—chief of them being Lugalzagesi of Uruk—who actively competed among themselves for the hegemony over southern Babylonia.[61] The decision of Urukagina to become a lugal, and the fact that, as it is clear, he considerably expanded royal control over temple households during his reign—which of course constituted a direct violation of his electoral promises—should be evaluated in this light.[62] As is well known, of course, even if these actions were forced upon him by the exigencies of foreign politics—rather than having been motivated by his personal ambitions—they ended in total failure.

Thus, the mystery of Urukagina continues. Was he a cynical populist, who promised to restore the values of the past ("to make Sumer great again") and to cut taxes, and then, once elected, he ruthlessly abandoned those ideals and promises, surpassing his predecessors in his lust for power? Or was he an earnest reformer, who was defeated by the political circumstances independent of his intentions? We will probably never know for certain.

60 A similar project had been undertaken, following the fall of the Sargonic Empire, by Gudea, who too attempted to restore the ideals of the temple-community in Lagaš. This project likewise proved unsuccessful, though Gudea's intentions may have been more sincere than those of Urukagina. See Steinkeller 2017a, 32–34.

61 All of whom, not by accident, were lugals.

62 In my view, this is reflected in the fact that Urukagina expanded the personnel of the House of the Woman (e_2-mi_2) during his reign. See Maekawa 1973–1974, 136, 139–140. Although renamed as the household of Bau by Urukagina, this institution continued to be controlled by him and his family. The same was true of the household of Ningirsu, which had been turned by Lugalanda (or already by En-entarzi) into the ensik's "palace"; Steinkeller 2019, 127–128. Here it is significant that Urukagina did not restore its original name, e_2 ^{d}Nin-gir_2-su. In this connection, equally telling is the fact that Urukagina increased the numbers of the RU-lugal people and aga_3-us_2, "elite soldiers, guards," who, as it may safely be conjectured, constituted military personnel directly subordinated to, and economically dependent on the ruler of Lagaš. See Selz 1995, 56; id. 2014, 261–262; Prentice 2010, 71; Schrakamp 2014. For the RU-lugal and aga_3-us_2 serving as soldiers, see DP 138 (year Urukagina L 4?), which lists thirty-one dead men, respectively divided into RU-lugal-me (vi 1) and aga_3-us_2-me (viii 2). Cf. Selz 1995, 81 [174]. As shown by the spellings RU-lugal-ke_4 (Ukg 1 vii 17, Ukg 3 ii 4′), RU-lugal-ke_4-ne (DP 641 iii 1), and 3 PNs ugula RU-lugal-ke_4-ne-me /ugula RU-lugal-ak-ene-ak-me(š)/ (VAS 27 9 ii 4–iii 1),

Appendix

Text 1 (VAS 27 33 = VAT 4735; Undated, Lugalanda Year 6 or 7)

i

1) 1(ul) še 1(ul) ziz$_2$
2) Gir$_3$-ni
3) sanga-GAR-ka
4) 3(ban$_2$) še 3(ban$_2$) ziz$_2$
5) ama dub-sar
6) 3(ban$_2$) še 3(ban$_2$) ziz$_2$
7) Bi-su-ga$_2$
8) 1(ul) še 1(ul) ziz$_2$ Ušur$_3$-ama-mu
9) 3(ban$_2$) še 3(ban$_2$) ziz$_2$
10) Tul$_2$-ta
11) dam Ur-ka$_2$
12) 3(ban$_2$) še 3(ban$_2$) ziz$_2$
13) dam Ki-tuš-lu$_2$

ii

1) 3(ban$_2$) še 3(ban$_2$) ziz$_2$ Me
2) 1(ul) še 1(ul) ⸢ziz$_2$ Ur⸣-^{d}Ba-u$_2$
3) 1(ul) še 1(ul) ⸢ziz$_2$⸣ [Ig]i-zi
4) 2(ul) še 2(ul) ziz$_2$
5) U$_2$-u$_2$-ur$_2$
6) gal-uku$_3$
7) 3(ban$_2$) še 3(ban$_2$) ziz$_2$
8) Bur$_5$^{mušen}-tur
9) 1(ul) še 1(ul) ziz$_2$ dam Ur-^{d}⸢Nin-pirig⸣
10) 3(ban$_2$) še 3(ban$_2$) ziz$_2$
11) Barag-a
12) 3(ban$_2$) še 3(ban$_2$) ziz$_2$

iii

1) ⸢x⸣-mu-za?
2) 3(ban$_2$) še 3(ban$_2$) ziz$_2$

RU-lugal is a genitival construction. The most likely analysis of this term is šub-lugal / šub-lugal-ak/ "the subject of the master/king," where šub means "to cast, to subject (oneself) down." As such, šub-lugal would be a Sumerian equivalent of the Akkadian *muškēnu*, "the one who prostrates/submits himself."

3) ⸢dumu⸣ Lugal-ra
4) 3(ban$_2$) še 3(ban$_2$) ziz$_2$
5) dumu Nir-gal$_2$
6) 1(ul) še 1(ul) ziz$_2$
7) Nar$_x$(RSP-468bis)
8) engar
9) 2(ul) še 2(ul) ziz$_2$ ^{d}Ba-u$_2$
10) ašgab
11) 1(ul) še 1(ul) ziz$_2$ ⸢Nigar$_x$-mud⸣
12) ⸢taka$_4$⸣-alam
13) 3(ban$_2$) še 3(ban$_2$) ziz$_2$ Amar-^{d}Hendur
14) zadim

iv
1) ⸢3(ban$_2$) še⸣ 3(ban$_2$) ziz$_2$ Ka-tar
2) Lugal-nig$_2$-gur$_8$
3) ⸢3(ban$_2$) še⸣ 3(ban$_2$) ziz$_2$ ama Ur-HAR
4) 1(ul) še 1(ul) ziz$_2$
5) Ur-HAR-ra
6) 3(ban$_2$) še 3(ban$_2$) ziz$_2$
7) ⸢Nigir⸣-abzu
8) nu-kiri$_6$
9) 3(ban$_2$) še 3(ban$_2$) ziz$_2$
10) dam Lugal-ra
11) 3(ban$_2$) še 3(ban$_2$) ziz$_2$ Nin-e$_2$-gissun-na
12) 2(ul) še 2(ul) ziz$_2$
13) U$_2$-u$_2$
14) gir$_4$-bil

v
1) ⸢3(ban$_2$) še 3(ban$_2$) ziz$_2$⸣
2) Geme$_2$-Ba
3) dumu A-i$_3$-li$_2$
4) ⸢2(ul)⸣ še 2(ul) ziz$_2$
5) Gan-Ba
6) 1(ul) še 1(ul) ziz$_2$
7) Amar-ezem
8) 1(ul) še 1(ul) ziz$_2$ ⸢Gir$_2$⸣-[n]un
9) 1(ul) še 1(ul) ziz$_2$ Sig$_4$-zi
10) ⸢2(ul) še⸣ 2(ul) ziz$_2$ Gu-ni

11) nagar
12) 3(ban$_2$) še 3(ban$_2$) ziz$_2$
13) Ama-AB
14) kar-ke$_4$(KID)

vi
1) 3(ban$_2$) še 3(ban$_2$) ziz$_2$
2) Pu$_3$-za
3) erased
4) 3(ban$_2$) še 3(ban$_2$) ziz$_2$ A-DU.DU-še$_3$
5) 3(ban$_2$) še 3(ban$_2$) ziz$_2$
6) Nin-⸢ ...⸣
7) 3(ban$_2$) še 3(ban$_2$) ziz$_2$
8) Gan-e$_2$
9) 1(ul) še 1(ul) ziz$_2$
10) Amar-ezem
11) bahar$_2$

vii
1) 3(ban$_2$) še 3(ban$_2$) ziz$_2$
2) dam Za-u$_2$
3) šu-ku$_6$
4) 1(ul) še 1(ul) ziz$_2$
5) Nin-ezem-ma-ni
6) 1(ul) še 1(ul) ziz$_2$
7) nin Mu-a
8) 3(ban$_2$) še 3(ban$_2$) ziz$_2$ dumu Mu-a
9) 1(ul) še 1(ul) ziz$_2$
10) Ki-tuš-lu$_2$
11) muhaldim
12) 1(ul) [še] 1(ul) ziz$_2$
13) [...]

viii
1) 1(ul) še 1(ul) ziz$_2$
2) nu-gig
3) 1(ul) še 1(ul) ziz$_2$
4) munu$_4$-mu$_2$
5) 3(ban$_2$) še 3(ban$_2$) ziz$_2$
6) E$_2$-lu$_2$

ix
1) šu-nigin$_2$ 25(gur) še gur-2-ul [= 1,800 liters]
2) 25(gur) ziz$_2$ [= 1,800 liters]
3) ziz$_2$-ba še-ba
4) ušur$_3$-ne
5) Uru-ka
6) gal-uku$_3$-ke$_4$
7) ezem ^{d}Ba-u$_2$-ka

x
1) e-ne-ba

Text 2 (DP 128; Year Urukagina L 2)

i
1) 1(ul) ziz$_2$-ba
2) Gir$_3$-ni-ba-dab$_5$
3) šeš sanga-GAR
4) 1(ul) Nam-dumu
5) ama dub-sar
6) 3(ban$_2$) Bi-su-ga$_2$
7) nig$_2$-DIN
8) 3(ban$_2$) Tul$_2$-ta
9) dam Ur-ka$_2$-tur
10) 3(ban$_2$) E$_2$-ul-li

ii
1) dam Ki-tuš-lu$_2$
2) 3(ban$_2$) Bur$_5$^{mušen}-tur
3) 1(ul) dam Ur-^{d}Nin-pirig
4) sag-apin-ka
5) 3(ban$_2$) Barag-an-ni
6) 3(ban$_2$) Gan-ki
7) dam Lugal-ra
8) 3(ban$_2$) dumu Nir-gal$_2$
9) 3(ban$_2$) Nigar$_x$-mud

iii
1) taka$_4$-alan
2) 3(ban$_2$) Amar-^{d}Hendur
3) zadim

4) 3(ban$_2$) Ka-tar
5) dam Lugal-nig$_2$-gur$_8$
6) 3(ban$_2$) Ur-HAR-sar-ra
7) 3(ban$_2$) Ar$_3$-tu
8) ama Ur-HAR-sar-ra-ka
9) 3(ban$_2$) Nin-e$_2$-⸢gissun⸣-ni
10) 3(ban$_2$) Geme$_2$-^{d}Ba-u$_2$

iv

1) dumu A-i$_3$-li$_2$
2) 3(ban$_2$) Ama-AB-e$_2$-ta
3) kar-ke$_3$(AK)
4) 3(ban$_2$) U$_2$-za
5) 3(ban$_2$) Ur-šu
6) dal-mušen
7) 3(ban$_2$) Nin-šag$_4$-la$_2$-tuku
8) 3(ban$_2$) Gan-e$_2$
9) 3(ban$_2$) dam Za-u$_2$
10) šu-ku$_6$
11) 3(ban$_2$) nin Mu-an-ni-dug$_4$

v

1) 3(ban$_2$) dumu Mu-an-ni-dug$_4$
2) 1(ul) Ki-tuš-lu$_2$
3) lu$_2$-sar
4) 1(ul) Amar-ezem
5) bahar$_2$
6) 1(ul) Gan-ezem
7) dam Lugal-eš$_3$-e$_3$-ka
8) 3(ban$_2$) Nam-šita! (copy: TUR)
9) i$_3$-du$_8$

vi

1) 1(ul) Lum-ma-gur$_7$
2) ašgab
3) 1(ul) En-ki-nu-nir-ki-dug$_3$
4) ugula
5) 1(ul) Gan-ezem
6) nu-gig
7) 1(ul) dam E$_2$-ki-gal-la

8) nu-banda$_3$
9) 1(ul) En-DU

vii
1) GAM.GAM
2) 2(ul) Ur-^{d}Ba-u$_2$
3) ašgab

viii
1) šu-nigin$_2$ 5(gur) 2(ul) ziz$_2$ gur-sag-gal$_2$ [= 792 liters]
2) ziz$_2$-ba ušur$_3$ nam-dumu
3) Sag$_9$-sag$_9$
4) dam Uru-ka-gi-na
5) lugal
6) Lagaš^{ki}-ka-me

ix
1) ezem ^{d}Ba-u$_2$-ka
2) En-ig-gal
3) nu-banda$_3$
4) e$_2$-ezem-da Uru-kug-ga-ta
5) e-ne-ba 2

Text 3 (DP 129; Year Urukagina L 3)

i
1) 1(ul) ziz$_2$-ba
2) Gir$_3$-ni-ba-dab$_5$
3) šeš sanga-GAR
4) 1(ul) Nam-dumu
5) ama dub-sar
6) 3(ban$_2$) Bi-su-ga$_2$
7) nig$_2$-DIN
8) 3(ban$_2$) Tul$_2$-ta
9) dam Ur-ka$_2$-tur
10) 3(ban$_2$) E$_2$-ul-li

ii
1) dam Ki-tuš-lu$_2$
2) 3(ban$_2$) Bur$_5$^{mušen}-tur
3) 1(ul) dam Ur-^{d}Nin-pirig

4) sag-apin-ka
5) 3(ban$_{2}$) Barag-an-ni
6) 3(ban$_{2}$) Gan-ki
7) dam Lugal-ra
8) 3(ban$_{2}$) dumu Nir-gal$_{2}$
9) 3(ban$_{2}$) Nigar$_{3}$-mud
10) taka$_{4}$-alam

iii

1) 3(ban$_{2}$) Amar-^{d}Hendur
2) zadim
3) 3(ban$_{2}$) Ka-tar
4) dam Lugal-nig$_{2}$-gur$_{8}$
5) 3(ban$_{2}$) Ur-HAR-sar-ra
6) 3(ban$_{2}$) Geme$_{2}$-^{d}Ba-u$_{2}$
7) dumu A-i$_{3}$-li$_{2}$
8) 3(ban$_{2}$) Ama-AB-e$_{2}$-ta
9) kar-ke$_{3}$(AK)
10) 3(ban$_{2}$) U$_{2}$-za
11) 3(ban$_{2}$) Ur-šu

iv

1) dal-mušen
2) 3(ban$_{2}$) Gan-e$_{2}$
3) 3(ban$_{2}$) nin Mu-an-ni-dug$_{4}$
4) 3(ban$_{2}$) dumu Mu-an-ni-dug$_{4}$
5) 1(ul) Ki-tuš-lu$_{2}$
6) lu$_{2}$-sar
7) 1(ul) Amar-ezem
8) bahar$_{2}$
9) 1(ul) Gan-ezem
10) dam Lugal-eš$_{3}$-e$_{3}$-ka

v

1) 3(ban$_{3}$) Nam-šita-mu-bi$_{2}$-dug$_{4}$
2) i$_{3}$-du$_{8}$
3) 3(ban$_{2}$) Lum-ma-gur$_{7}$
4) ašgab
5) 3(ban$_{3}$) En-ki-nu-nir-ki-dug$_{3}$
6) ugula

7) 3(ban$_2$) Gan-ezem
8) nu-gig
9) 3(ban$_2$) dam E$_2$-ki-gal-la

vi

1) nu-banda$_3$
2) 3(ban$_2$) En-DU
3) GAM.GAM
4) 2(ul) Ur-^{d}Ba-u$_2$
5) ašgab
6) 3(ban$_2$) Munus-sag$_9$-ga
7) dam Lugal-ušur$_3$-ra
8) sag-apin-ka
9) 3(ban$_2$) Za-u$_2$
10) šu-ku$_6$

vii

1) šu-nigin$_2$ 5(gur) 1(ul) 4(ban$_3$) ziz$_2$ gur-sag-gal$_2$ [= 780 liters]
2) ziz$_2$-ba ušur$_3$ nam-dumu
3) Sag$_9$-sag$_9$
4) dam Uru-ka-gi-na
5) lugal
6) Lagaš^{ki}-ka-me

viii

1) ezem ^{d}Ba-u$_2$-ka
2) En-ig-gal
3) nu-banda$_3$
4) e$_2$-ezem-da Uru-kug-ga-ta
5) e-ne-ba 3

Excursus: udu had_2/ha-ad in Urukagina's "Reforms"

In three passages of the "Reforms," wooly sheep are designated as had_2(UD):

(1) Ukg 1 iii 18–iv 1

sipad udu-siki-ka-ke_4-ne bar udu had_2-ka kug bi-gar-re_2-$eš_2$

The shepherds of wooly sheep had to substitute silver for the had_2 sheep (i.e., if the sheep were had_2).[63]

(2) Ukg 1 viii 28–ix 1

bar udu had_2-ka bar $sila_4$ gaba-ka-ka kug-a ga_2-ga_2-da maškim-bi e-šub

He abolished the requirement (lit.: the bailiff) of substituting silver because of the had_2 sheep and the ... lambs.

(3) Ukg. 3 i 11′–21′

[agrig-g]e-ne ugula-ugula-ne gala-e-ne engar-re_2-ne lu_2-$BAPPIR_3$ -ke_4-ne udu-siki u_3-mu-de_6 e_2-gal-la u_3-ur_4 ud-da udu e-had_2 siki-bi e_2-gal-la a-ba-de_6 kug 5 gin_2-am_6 e-ga_2-ga_2-ne

When stewards, foremen, lamentation priests, chief farmers, and brewers brought in wooly sheep (they owed to the ensik), and when they were then shorn in the "palace," if (any of those) sheep were had_2, after their wool was taken away in the "palace," they had to substitute 5 shekels of silver (per sheep).

This term also appears in a Pre-Sargonic Lagaš tablet published by Foxvog (1994, 11), henceforth the Foxvog Tablet. It dates to year Lugalanda 4:

i 1) 4 udu siki ha-ad
2) $Nigar_x$-mud
3) 1 ⌜udu Ur-urin-du_3-a⌝

63 Here and in passages (2) and (3), kug(-a) gar means "to substitute silver (for something),"

ii 1) $ensi_2$-k[e_4]
2) udu-⌜siki ud⌝ ur_4-r[a]
3) ⌜zag⌝ šu[š-a]
iii 1) kug 5 gin_2-ta
2) gu_2-ne-ne-a
3) e-ne-⌜gar⌝
4) Barag-na[m-tar]-ra
iv 1) dam Lugal-an-da
2) $ensi_2$
3) Lagaš^{ki}-ka 4

4 had_2 wooly sheep: Ningarmud; 1 (had_2 wooly sheep): Ur-urindua. When the wooly sheep were shorn (and) branded, the ensik charged them 5 shekels for each (sheep). (Under the authority of) Barag-namtara, wife of Lugalanda, ensik of Lagaš. (Year) 4.

As already recognized by Foxvog, this unique record is directly related to the "Reforms" passages in question. Both Ningarmud and Ur-urindua are otherwise known to have been shepherds (sipad) in charge of wooly sheep.[64] This agrees with passage (1), which likewise deals with the had_2 animals in care of the shepherds of wooly sheep. Also, the fact that these two individuals had to pay 5 shekels of silver for each had_2 sheep to the "palace" agrees with passage (3), where the identical fee due to the "palace" is specified.

Because of the syllabic spelling ha-ad in Foxvog Tablet i 1 and DP 258 i 5 (for which see below), it is certain that, in this context, the sign UD is to be read had_2. This brings us to the meaning of had_2. Assuming that had_2 describes the quality of wool, Foxvog (1994, 12–13) speculated that its meaning is "pure." But this is impossible for two reasons. First, the wording of passages (1), (2), (3), and the Foxvog Tablet makes it clear that had_2 does not describe the wool but the sheep *themselves*. And second, the five shekels of silver charged by the "palace" for each had_2 sheep obviously constituted a penalty. Therefore, had_2 must denote something undesirable, thus excluding the meaning "pure" or any other desirable quality or condition.

In my opinion, a much better solution is that had_2 corresponds here to UD(.DA), likely to be read had_2(-da) = Akkadian *ṣētu*, a sickness caused by

lit: "to replace in/with silver." I base this conclusion on the use of gar in DP 258 and VAS 14 73 (for which see below), where gar clearly means "to substitute, to replace."

64 Foxvog 1994, 11; Balke 2017, 311–312, 450.

exposure to sun or heat.[65] If so, the penalty in question was levied on the shepherd (or the sheep's caretaker as in passage 3, above) when the animals in his care died of heat stress, i.e., hyperthermia.[66] Accordingly, the closest translation of had_2 possible would be "to become dehydrated, dehydration."[67]

These facts argue that the loss of animals due to heat stress was treated as a case of the shepherd's negligence, and that, therefore, he was financially culpable for it. As described in passage (3) and the Foxvog Tablet, this would happen at the yearly shearing of the ensik's sheep, which were brought to the "palace" for this occasion by the shepherds, as well as by other parties owing sheep to the ensik. If any of the sheep had died of heat stress prior to that event, the shepherds and the other parties would produce the dead sheep's wool, which likely came together with their hides.[68] In addition, they would pay the said penalty.

That the had_2 sheep represented dead animals is confirmed by the texts recording replacements of such sheep: 2 udu-siki lul-gu-ak (udu-)siki ha-ad-kam ba-gar $Nigar_x$-mud, "2 wooly sheep were substituted by Nigarmud (as) a replacement (lul-gu-ak) for the wooly had_2 (sheep)" (DP 258 i 3–ii 1; year Urukagina E 1); 2 udu-siki lul-gu-ak (udu-)siki had_2-kam … ba-gar $Nigar_x$-mud (VAS 14 73 i 3–ii 3; year Lugalanda 5); 1 udu siki lul-gu-ak (udu-)siki had_2-kam … ba-gar Ur-urin-du_3-a (ibid. ii 6–iii 4).[69] Note that

65 CAD Ṣ: 153. Another term for this condition could be the Old Babylonian *pissatu* disease, which afflicted sheep and cattle. According to "Hammurabi Code" § 267, and herding contracts, cited in CAD P: 245–246, if any of the animals died from *pissatu* due to the negligence of the shepherd, the shepherd was responsible for their restitution. Note that while the negligent shepherd was required to replace the dead animals, he was not liable for pecuniary damages, as was the case in the "Reforms."

66 Although hyperthermia may affect any breed of sheep, it is more common among wooly sheep, particularly when their coats are dark and thick, which are more likely to accumulate heat. See Veterinary Handbook, n.d. "Disease: Heat Stress". Accessed March 17, 2022. http://www.veterinaryhandbook.com.au.

67 This sense derives from the basic meaning of had_2, which is "dried (out), withered, desiccated." See the Ur III terms: geštin had_2, "raisins" (*passim*); esir had_2, "dried bitumen" (*passim*), 2 udu niga uzu had_2-$še_3$, "2 grain-fed sheep for dried meat" (Ontario 1 48:4); etc. For had_2 as a verb, see "Gudea Cylinder A" xix 3: u_3-šub mu-dub_2 sig_4 had_2-de_3 ba-šub, "he struck the brick mold and the brick fell down for drying."

68 In Ur III times, when sheep, cattle, and donkeys died of natural causes, the shepherds and other persons responsible for them were customarily required to take an assertory oath (nam-$erem_2$) to that effect. In addition, they produced, partly for evidentiary reasons, hides of the dead animals. See, e.g., Aleppo 408; HSS 4 42; MTB 237; MCS 6 2 BM 100439; MVN 3 373; Nebraska 44 iv 22; Nisaba 33 760; SET 310 iii 22–25; etc. Cf. also "Hammurabi Code" § 266, cited below n. 72.

69 For the had_2 sheep being dead, see also the following passage: 2 $maš_2$ udu had_2-da-

Nigarmud and Ur-urindua are the same persons as the two shepherds appearing in the Foxvog Tablet.

Losses of cattle due to heat stress and similar causes were also subject to penalties. This is illustrated by the text DP 103, dated to year Urukagina E 1:

i
1) 1 gir mu 1
2) gir DUN-a
3) Dingir-šeš-mu
4) unud-kam
5) ^{d}Nin-gir$_2$-su-lu$_2$-mu

ii
1) dal-mušen-da
2) na ba-da-ri
3) kug-bi 10 gin$_2$
4) Sag$_9$-sag$_9$

iii
1) dam Uru-ka-gi-na
2) ensi$_2$
3) Lagaš^{ki}-ka-ra
4) e$_2$-gal-la

iv
1) šu-na i$_3$-ni-gi$_4$ 1

> 1 one-year-old heifer, a heifer under the authority of Dingir-šešmu, the cowherd, was 'smitten' (while) being with Ningirsu-lumu, the bird chaser. Its (penalty) of 10 shekels of silver was paid to (lit.: entered the hand of) Sagsag, wife of Urukagina, ensik of Lagaš in the "palace." (Year) 1.

For na ... ri(-g)/de$_5$(-g), "to fell (a tree, etc.), to be smitten/stricken, to fall (of animals)," see most recently Sallaberger (2005).[70] A related term is Ur III

kam ... Ur-^{d}En-ki-ke$_4$ mu-lah$_4$ ab-ku$_2$, "2 goats, among the had$_2$ sheep, were delivered by Ur-Enki; they were consumed" (OSP 1 106 i 1–ii 2; Pre-Sargonic, Nippur; courtesy of M. Molina).

70 Sallaberger 2005, 242–244, translates na ... ri(-g) in such Pre-Sargonic contexts as "to be cleared away." But the translation "to be smitten" fits much better in all the examples cited

and Old Babylonian ri-ri-ga, "fallen (animals)," Akkadian *miqittu* (Hh XIII 20 = MSL 8/2 9; CAD M/2 101–102). In Ur III sources, one also finds a_2-sig_3 ri-ri-ga, "(animals) fallen by a_2-sig_3."[71]

The term a_2 sig_3(-a) means "stricken by the (supernatural) arm."[72]

As I understand DP 103, the heifer in care of the cowherd Dingir-šešmu died (likely of heat stress) while being with the bird chaser Dingirsu-lumu. The latter person probably was pasturing the animal. Consequently, the cowherd paid to the "palace" 10 shekels of silver as a penalty. Not unexpectedly, the penalty was twice as large as that paid for sheep in the Foxvog Tablet.

As demonstrated by the Foxvog Tablet, in agreement with Urukagina's "Reforms," Lugalanda indeed charged shepherds 5 shekels of silver for each wooly sheep lost due to heat stress. This fact is very important, for it lends at least some credence to that document. However, we lack evidence that would allow us to verify if this penalty was in fact abolished by Urukagina. Since at least during the first year of his reign Urukagina continued to charge shepherds for the identical losses of cattle (see DP 103 discussed above), chances are that it was not.

---

by Sallaberger. Note that he himself concludes that the animals so designated were dead (id., 244). That na … ri(-g) is semantically the same as ri-ri-ga, see udu na-ri-ga, preceded by udu ri-ri-ga in OB Nippur Ura 03 lines 19–20 (DCCLT). And note the following Ur III examples: 1 $maš_2$ ma_2-e na ri-ga, "1 goat was stricken by a boat" (SACT 2 268:1–2); 1 udu bar-ba zi-ga ma_2-e na ri-ga, "1 sheep, its fleece has been removed, was stricken by a boat" (SNAT 409 i 6–7). In at least one instance (YOS 4 204), ri-ri-ga is applied also to humans: 3 dead men ri-ri-ga.

71 For the examples, see BDTNS, under a_2-sag_3. Note also: 2 u_8 a_2-si-ga 1 uz_3 a_2-si-ga (StrKT 45:1–2); 2 u_8 a_2-si-ga 1 uz_3 a_2-si-ga (YOS 15 158 iii 6–7, ix 9, 14; courtesy of M. Molina); animals ba-ug_7 a_2-sig_3, "dead from a_2-sig_3" (MVN 4 79:9; etc.); 3 $šah_2$ u_2 ri-ri-ga gir_3 a_2-sig_3, "3 grass-fed pigs, stricken on the road by a_2-sig_3" (AOS 32 W34:1–3; courtesy of M. Molina); PN a_2-sig_3 ba-an-s[ig_3]-a, "(because) PN_1 was stricken by a_2-sig_3 (PN_2 appeared in court in his place)" (ITT 3 6550:5–7); a_2 tu-ra a_2-sig_3 gal_2-la, "workdays (of women) sick from a_2-sig_3" (UET 9 325 v' 7'). a_2-sig_3 is likely identical with the demon A_2-sag_3, Akkadian *Asakku*.

72 Cf. "Hammurabi Code" § 266: *šum-ma i-na* TUR_3 *li-pí-it* DINGIR *it-tab-ši ù lu* UR.MAH *id-du-ak* SIPAD *ma-ḫar* DINGIR *ú-ub-ba-am-ma mi-qí-it-ti* TUR_3 *be-el* TUR_3 *i-maḫ-ḫar-šu*, "if the 'touch of the god' happens in the fold, or if a lion kills (any animals), the shepherd will clear himself before the god (by taking an assertory oath), and the owner of the fold will be responsible for the fallen (animals) in the fold." Cf. also "the striking hand of God" as the term for leprosy in the Bible.

References

Alster, Bendt. 1997. *Proverbs of Ancient Sumer*. Bethesda MD: CDL.

Balke, Thomas. 2017. *Das altsumerische Onomastikon. Namengebung und Prosopografie nach den Quellen aus Lagas*. dubsar 1. Münster: Zaphon.

Civil, Miguel. 1983. "An Early Dynastic School Exercise from Lagaš (Al-Hiba 29)." *BiOr* 40: 559–566.

Civil, Miguel (2008), *The Early Dynastic Practical Vocabulary A (Archaic HAR-ra A)*. ARES 4. Rome: Missione Archeologica Italiana in Syria.

Everest-Phillips, Max. 2018. *The Passionate Bureaucrat: Lessons for 21st Century from 4,500 Years of Public Service Reform*. Singapore: World Scientific Publishing.

Foxvog, Daniel A. 1994. "A New Lagaš Text Bearing on Uruinimgina's Reforms." *JCS* 46: 11–15.

Frayne, Douglas R. 1993. *Sargonic and Gutian Periods (2334–2113 BC)*. RIME 2. Toronto: University of Toronto.

Frayne, Douglas R. 2008. *Pre-Sargonic Period (2700–2350 BC)*. RIME 1. Toronto: University of Toronto.

Maeda, Tohru. 1982. "Subgroups of lú-KUR$_6$-dab$_5$-ba (I)—sag-dub and šeš-bìr-ra." *ASJ* 4: 69–84.

Maeda, Tohru. 1983. "Subgroups of lú-KUR$_6$-dab$_5$-ba (II)—šeš-gub-ba and šeš-tuš-a." *ASJ* 5: 67–79.

Maekawa, Kazuya. 1973–1974. "The Development of the é-mí in Lagash during Early Dynastic III." *Mesopotamia* 8/9: 77–144.

Marzahn, Joachim. 1996. *Altsumerische Verwaltungstexte und ein Brief aus Girsu/Lagaš*. VAS 27. Mainz: von Zabern.

Prentice, Rosemary. 2010. *The Exchange of Goods and Services in Pre-Sargonic Lagash*. AOAT 368. Münster: Ugarit Verlag.

Sallaberger, Walther. 2005. "The Sumerian Verb na de$_5$(-g) 'To Clear.'" In *"An Experienced Scribe Who Neglects Nothing." Ancient Near Eastern Studies in Honor of Jacob Klein*, Edited by Yitzhak Sefati, Pinhas Artzi, Chaim Cohen, Barry L. Eichler, Victor Hurowitz, 229–253. Bethesda MD: CDL.

Sallaberger, Walther and Ingo Schrakamp. 2015. "Philological Data for a Historical Chronology of M esopotamia in the 3rd Millennium." In *History & Philology*. ARCANE III, edited by Walther Sallaberger and Ingo Schrakamp, 1–136. Turhout: Brepols.

Schrakamp, Ingo. 2014. "Krieger un Bauern: RU-lugal und aga$_3$/aga-us$_2$ im Militär des altsumerischen Lagaš." In *Krieg und Frieden im Alten Vorderasien, 52e Rencontre Assyriologique Internationale, Münster, 17.–21. Juli 2006*, AOAT 401, edited by Manfred Dietrich and Hans Neumann, 445–465. Münster: Ugarit Verlag.

Schrakamp, Ingo. 2015. "Urukagina und die Geschichte von Lagaš am Ende der Präsargonischen Zeit." In *It's a Long Way to a Historiography of the Early Dynastic Period(s)*, Altertumskunde des Vorderen Orients 15, edited by Reinhard Dittmann, Gebhard J. Selz, and Ellen Rehm, 303–385. Münster: Ugarit Verlag.

Selz, Gebhard. 1995. *Untersuchungen zur Götterwelt des altsumerischen Stadtstaates von Lagaš*, Occasional Publications of the Samuel Noah Kramer Fund 13. Philadelphia.

Selz, Gebhard. 1999–2000. "'Wirtschaftskrise—Legitimationskrise—Staatskrise.' Zur Genese mesopotamischer Rechtvorstellungn zwischen Planwirtschaft und Eigentumsverfassung." *AfO* 46/47: 1–44.

Selz, Gebhard. 2014. "Einer Sozialgeschichte der spätfrühdynastischen Zeit. Das Beispiel Lagas, oder: 'The Inhabited Ghosts of Our Intellectual Ancestors'." In *Studies in Economic and Social History in Memory of Péter Vargyas*. Ancient Near Eastern and Mediterranean Studies 2, edited by Zoltán Csabai, 239–281. Pécs; Budapest: Department of Ancient History, University of Pécs: L'Harmattan; Kiadó, 2014.

Steible, Horst. 1983. *Glossar zu den altsumerischen Bau- und Weihinschriften*. FAOS 6. Stuttgart: Franz Steiner.

Steinkeller, Piotr. 1978. "On the Reading and Meaning of a-ZAR-la." *RA* 72: 73–76.

Steinkeller, Piotr. 1989. *Sale Documents of the Ur III Period*. FAOS 17. Stuttgart: Franz Steiner.

Steinkeller, Piotr. 1991. "The Reforms of UruKAgina and an Early Sumerian Term for 'Prison.'" In *Velles Paraules: Ancient Near Eastern Studies in Honor of Miguel Civil*. Aula Orientalis 9, edited by Piotr Michalowski. et al., 227–233, Barcelona: AUSA.

Steinkeller, Piotr. 1993. "Early Political Development in Mesopotamia and the Origins of the Sargonic Empire." In *Akkad: The First World Empire: Structure, Ideology, Traditions*, History of the Ancient Near East / Studies 5, edited by Mario Liverani, 107–129. Padua: Sargon srl.

Steinkeller, Piotr. 1995. "Sheep and Goat Terminology in Ur III Sources from Drehem." *Bulletin on Sumerian Agriculture* 8: 49–70.

Steinkeller, Piotr. 1999. "On Rulers, Priests and Sacred Marriage: Tracing the Evolution of Early Sumerian Kingship." *In Priests and Officials in the Ancient Near East: Papers of the Second Colloquium on the Ancient Near East—The City and its Life Held at the Middle Eastern Culture Center in Japan (Mitaka, Tokyo) March, 22–24, 1996*, edited by Kazuko Watanabe, 103–137. Heidelberg: C. Winter.

Steinkeller, Piotr. 2013. "An Archaic 'Prisoner Plaque' from Kiš." *RA* 107: 131–157.

Steinkeller, Piotr. 2017a. *History, Texts and Art in Early Babylonia: Three Essays*. SANER 15. Berlin: de Gruyter.

Steinkeller, Piotr. 2017b. "Luck, Fortune and Destiny in Ancient Mesopotamia—Or How the Sumerians and Babylonians Thought of Their Place in the Flow of Things." In *Fortune and Misfortune in the Ancient Near East, Proceedings of the 60th Rencontre Assyriologique Internationale at Warsaw, 21–25 July 2014*, edited by Olga Drewnowska and Małgorzata Sandowicz, 5–24. Winona Lake IN: Eisenbrauns.

Steinkeller, Piotr. 2019. "Babylonian Priesthood during the Third Millennium BCE: Between Sacred and Profane," *JANER* 19: 112–151.

Steinkeller, Piotr. Forthcoming. "On Prostitutes, Alewives, and Midwives in Third Millennium Babylonia."

Steinkeller, Piotr. Unpublished manuscript. "Residence Patterns and Population Density in the City of Umma at ca. 2000 BC". Presented at the Università di Roma "La Sapienza," May 10, 2013.

Visicato, Giuseppe. 1997. *Indices of Early Dynastic Administrative Tablets of Šuruppak.* Istituto Universitario Orientale di Napoli, Dipartimento di Studi Asiatici, Series Maior VI/A. Naples.

Vukosavović, Filip. 2008. "A New 'Reform Text' of Uruinimgina: Ukg 63." *RA* 102: 8.

CHAPTER 2

Samsuiluna and the Reconquest of Nippur

Nathan Steinmeyer | ORCID: 0000-0001-9159-9431
Tel Aviv University
steinmeyer@mail.tau.ac.il

Abstract

Despite the importance of the Late Old Babylonian Period (1711–1595 B.C.E.) for the reconstruction of the history of the second millennium and the collapse of the old Babylonian state, little is known about many of its features. This article seeks to fill in some of the gaps by investigating the conditions of Babylon's southern border which had shifted to the area around Nippur in the early years of King Samsuiluna's reign. Specifically, this study will examine the evidence for a possible dating of the reconquest of the city of Nippur—after its capture by Ilima-ilu of the First Sealand Dynasty. It will be suggested—based on year names and the mention of Ninurta's Udbanuil weapon in legal documents from Nippur and Dūr-Abiešuḫ—that this reconquest can be placed in Samsuiluna year 37. This suggestion must, however, remain merely a hypothesis until more conclusive evidence is found either way.

Keywords

Dūr-Abiešuḫ – Nippur – Samsuiluna – Late Old Babylonian Period – First Sealand Dynasty

תקציר

על אף חשיבותה של סוף התקופה הבבלית הקדומה (1711–1595 לפנה"ס) להבנת נפילת השושלת הראשונה של בבל, לא רב הידע באשר לתקופה זו. מאמר זה מנסה לענות על חלק מהשאלות הנוגעות לגבול הדרומי של ממלכת בבל, בסמוך לעיר ניפור, וזאת בשנים הראשונות של שלטונו של המלך סמסֻו-אילונה. המאמר בוחן את העדויות לתיארוך אפשרי של כיבושה מחדש של העיר ניפור—לאחר לכידתה על ידי אילימה-אילו מלך שושלת ארץ-הים. בהתבסס על כמה שמות שנים ועל איזכורו של כלי הנשק הטקסי אוּדבּנוּאיל אשר הוקדש לאל נינוּרתּ במסמכים משפטיים מניפור ומדור-אבי-אשוח, אני מציע לתארך את כיבושה מחדש של ניפור בשנה ה-37 למלכותו של סמסֻו-אילונה.

 | DOI:10.1163/9789004526822_003

מילות מפתח

דור-אבי-אשוח – ניפור – סמסו-אילונה – סוף התקופה הבבלית הקדומה – שושלת ארץ-הים א׳

المستخلص

على الرغم من أهمية نهاية الفترة البابلية القديمة (1711–1595 قبل الميلاد) لفهم سقوط السلالة البابلية الأولى ، لا يُعرف الكثير عن هذه الفترة. يحاول هذا المقال الإجابة عن بعض الأسئلة المتعلقة بالحدود الجنوبية لمملكة بابل التي انتقلت إلى منطقة مدينة نيبور خلال السنوات الأولى من حكم الملك سامسو إيلونا. يفحص المقال الأدلّة على التاريخ المحتمل لإعادة احتلال مدينة نيبور—بعد الاستيلاء عليها من قبل إيليما إيلو ملك سلالة القطر البحري. استنادًا إلى عدة أسماء للسنوات وذكر السلاح الاحتفالي أودبانويل المخصص للإله نينورتا في الوثائق القانونية من نيبور و دور-ابي-اشوخ ، أقترح أنّ إعادة احتلال نيبور حصلت في العام السابع والثلاثين من حكم سامسو إيلونا.

الكلمات المفتاحيّة

دور-ابي-اشوخ – نيبور – سامسو إيلونا – نهاية الفترة البابلية القديمة – سلالة القطر البحري

1 Introduction

The Late Old Babylonian Period stands as a transition between the apex of the Babylonian kingdom of Hammurāpi, and the succeeding Kassite dynasty.[1] However, despite the importance of this period on the history of the ancient Near East, little is known about its features outside of the major cities in the heartland.[2] This is especially true for the region of Central Babylonia. Until

1 Names in this work will be presented following standard conventions for each name, although more obscure individuals are generally presented with hyphenated names. Funding for this project was provided through a grant from the Israel Science Foundation (no. 1801/20) and the Chaim Rosenberg School of Jewish Studies-Archaeology, Tel Aviv University. My sincere gratitude to all the anonymous reviewers that helped me greatly improve this paper.

2 A few studies, such as Richardson 2002, have worked to solve this by examining the limited textual data from communities and fortresses outside of the major cities, but this has remained a minor feature in the study of the period.

recently, the evidence—both textually and archaeologically—pointed towards a loss of control and abandonment of Southern and Central Babylonia during the reign of Hammurāpi's son, Samsuiluna.[3] However, with the recent publications of tablets from Dūr-Abiešuḫ,[4] no longer is this theory of complete abandonment of Central Babylonia tenable.[5] Instead, what was revealed was the continued—and indeed persistent—presence of the Babylonian polity in Central Babylonia well into the reign of its last king, over a hundred years after the region was previously thought abandoned.

The publication of the Dūr-Abiešuḫ corpus has allowed scholars to fill in many gaps in the history of Central Babylonia. This paper seeks to continue that trend by proposing a solution to one of the remaining gaps. Specifically, this study will examine the evidence for a possible dating of the reconquest of the city of Nippur—after its capture by Ilima-ilu of the First Sealand Dynasty. It will be suggested—based on year names and the mention of Ninurta's Udbanuil weapon in legal documents from Nippur and Dūr-Abiešuḫ—that this reconquest can be placed in Samsuiluna year 37 (Si 37). This suggestion must, however, remain a hypothesis until more conclusive evidence is found either way.

2 Samsuiluna's Southern Problem

Before a discussion of the reconquest can begin, it is necessary to address the conflict that swept through Central Babylonia in the years immediately preceding the commencement of the Dūr-Abiešuḫ corpus.[6] The first blow against Babylon's power came in Si 8, after a rebellion swept from the south, northward. Texts dated with Babylonian year names cease in southern cities such as Larsa in Si 7 and do not reappear in many of them until Si 10.

---

3 E.g., Armstrong and Brandt 1994 or Stone 1977, for the archaeological evidence for the abandonment of Nippur during the reign of Samsuiluna. Gibson 1992, 44, however, suggested a small contingent of cultic officials could have remained in Nippur following the reign of Samsuiluna.

4 There are two sites in Central Babylonia known as Dūr-Abiešuḫ, "at the outlet of the Ḫammurabi-nuḫuš-nišī canal" and "at the Tigris-dam." See CUSAS 29 25, which mentions both forts. Since the present corpus originated from Dūr-Abiešuḫ at the outlet of the Ḫammurabi-nuḫuš-nišī canal, this fortress will simply be referred to as Dūr-Abiešuḫ.

5 Even before the publication of the Dūr-Abiešuḫ corpus, a few scholars had suggested from textual inferences that Babylon might have been able to regain Nippur following its capture by the First Sealand Dynasty. Cf. Frayne 1990, 425; Dalley 2009, 7–9.

6 See Zomer 2019, 3–15.

During the intervening years, texts are instead dated according to Rim-Sin II, who quickly gained control of much of the land of Sumer.[7] Yet, Rim-Sin's success was short-lived, and he was slain early in Si 9.[8] This was not the end of Samsuiluna's troubles, however, as he was forced to retake the region city by city.[9] It was not until early Si 10, that Samsuiluna was able to retake the city of Nippur, as attested by the return of Babylonian year names.[10] Yet this victory was limited, and by the end of the following year, Babylonian dated texts from nearly all southern cities stop.[11]

As Boivin (2018) has suggested, Samsuiluna's year names over the following decade are certainly evidence of a shift in Babylon's southern border.[12] His 15th year attested to his refortifying of Isin, and his 17th year to the construction of the fortress of Emutbalum.[13] Additionally, Samsuiluna's rebuilding of the wall of Nippur, attested in an undated inscription, is likely from this time as well.[14] Thus, in a period of ten years, Nippur and Central Babylonia had traded hands twice, as the region became the new border of a shrinking Babylonian state.

The next shockwave sent through Central Babylonia was the invasion of Ilima-ilu, the first king of the Sealand, around Si 29. Within a year, the entire region had once again slipped out of the control of Babylon. The latest texts dated from Isin come from Si 28. By Si 30, Lagaba and Maškan-Šapir had also descended into textual darkness.[15] Only Nippur gives a hint of the events that

7 Charpin 2004, 337–338. Several texts dated to this period have been excavated from Nippur, demonstrating Rim-Sin's control over the region; e.g., OECT 8 14 and 19.

8 The event is commemorated in an inscribed cylinder seal from Kiš; RIME 4 3.7.7.

9 Si 11 appears to be the end of this spurt of rebellions, as it is in this year that the walls of Ur and Uruk were destroyed; Zomer 2019, 4.

10 TIM 4 5 and 6. These are two duplicate legal texts from Nippur that date to the tenth month of Si 10.

11 Charpin 2004, 341–343.

12 Boivin 2018, 88, suggests that the rebuilding of the wall of Isin in the year name of Si 15, can be taken as evidence that Isin was being refortified to form a defensive line in Babylon's new southern border.

13 "The year: Samsuiluna, the king, (made firm again) the wall of Isin which had been destroyed, restored and (rebuilt) it"; Horsnell 1999, 201; and "The year: Samsuiluna, the king, (restored and rebuilt) the great fortress of Emutbalum which had been destroyed." Horsnell 1999, 204.

14 RIME 4 3.7.2. Despite its often-anachronistic nature, the statement in this text that Samsuiluna "caused the people of the land of Sumer and Akkad to dwell in peaceful abodes," could have been in reference to his reconquest of Southern and Central Babylonia following the rebellion of Rim-Sin II.

15 Charpin 2004, 360.

had transpired with the sudden appearance of texts dated to the reign of Ilima-ilu, demonstrating the king's control of the city for at least two years starting in late Si 30.[16]

Although the exact location and date of the First Sealand Dynasty's origin remain mysterious, the budding kingdom was able to build up its forces until—in one fell swoop—it amputated the entirety of Central Babylonia.[17] Thus, all Samsuiluna's efforts to fortify his new southern border were brought to naught, leaving practically no records of the event. One possible historical reference regarding Ilima-ilu's victories against Samsuiluna was recorded in a chronicle. The entry in the chronicle, however, is obscure and largely broken.[18]

3 The Evidence of the Dūr-Abiešuḫ Corpus

With this understanding, it is possible to begin examining the Dūr-Abiešuḫ corpus that today provides the majority of data regarding this region following the conquest of Nippur in Si 30. The first set of Dūr-Abiešuḫ texts were published by Karel Van Lerberghe and Gabriella Voet (2009).[19] The tablets all came from the antiquities market, likely looted in Iraq in the 1990s.[20] Despite being identified as originating from the Late Old Babylonian fortress of Dūr-Abiešuḫ—based on

16 My discussion will be treating Si 30 as the last year of Babylonian control of Nippur before it was taken by Ilima-ilu. However, there has been disagreement regarding the dating of the final Babylonian documents from Nippur. The main source of this problem is a group of eight texts from Nippur, bearing the year name "MU GIBIL 2.KAM.MA" without mention of a king: TMH 10 (??/i/-); 187 (??/iii/12); 178 (??/iii/21); 179 (??/iv/26); 141 (??/iii/23); 208 (??/i/2-); 180 (??/iv/-); and 186 (??/iii/2). Goddeeris 2016, 274–275 suggested that this year name is an abbreviation of Si 29. Meanwhile, Boivin 2018, 242 has suggested that this group should not be dated at all to the reign of Samsuiluna. Instead, the present study agrees with ARCHIBAB in dating the "MU GIBIL 2.KAM.MA" tablets to Si 30. The fact that these tablets all date to the first four months also fits well with the Ilima-ilu tablets, which first appear in the seventh month: SAOC 44 12; (Ii1/vii/16); TMH 10 54 (Ii1/ix/19); BE 6/2 68 (Ii2/viii/26); and PBS 8/1 89. This would leave a little under three months for the city of Nippur to trade hands.

17 Boivin 2018 and Zomer 2019.

18 "He built ... he did battle against him ... their corpses, the sea ... he *changed* and Samsu-Iluna ... Iliman (Ilima-ilu) attacked and [brought about] the defeat of [his] army"; TCS 5, Chronicle 20 B rev: 1–7.

19 CUSAS 8.

20 Földi 2017.

paleography, prosopography, internal evidence, and more—the lack of archaeological context has obscured the impact that this corpus has on reconstructions of the history of Central Babylonia, and it has made it difficult to state with certainty the exact location of Dūr-Abiešuḫ.[21]

Presently, 310 published tablets are proposed to originate from Dūr-Abiešuḫ.[22] These stretch from Abiešuḫ 4 to Samsuditana 15.[23] Following the modified Middle Chronology proposed by Richardson,[24] this would be a period of 96 years from 1708 B.C. to 1613 B.C. The overwhelming majority of these texts consist of administrative documents concerning the function of the fortress and the military and cultic staff located within it, as well as legal documents, letters, and more.[25] Several groups of tablets within this corpus deserve specific mention: ration documents, letters, records of the performance of extispicies, and the dossier of Enlil-mansum, the *nešakkum*-priest.

Both the ration documents and letters serve to demonstrate the continued presence of Babylonian troops within Nippur, Maškan-Šapir, and several other locations in Central Babylonia. One of the earliest documents within the corpus demonstrates this well. The document, dated to Ae 4, records the disbursement of rations for troops stationed at Dūr-Abiešuḫ, Birti-Nippur, and Dūr-Sinmuballiṭ.[26] Other documents mention rations for troops stationed at Kār-Nabium, Dūr-Abiešuḫ at the Tigris dam, Maškan-Šapir, Birti-Baganna, and more.[27] Several letters mention other forts controlled by the Babylonians as well.[28] The letter CUSAS 29 205 is especially interesting as it reports an attack

21 Van Lerberghe and Voet 2009, 4–6 originally suggested that Dūr-Abiešuḫ was located in Northern Babylonia, close to Harrādum. However, all preceding studies, including that of Abraham and Van Lerberghe 2017, have agreed that its location should be sought in the immediate vicinity of Nippur.

22 For the publication history of the Dūr-Abiešuḫ corpus, see the excursus, pp. 50–51. Another tablet has been identified by Béranger (2022), but awaits a full edition.

23 Abraham and Van Lerberge 2017, no. 160 = Ae 4; Sigrist, Gabbay, and Avila 2017, no. 5 = Sd 15.

24 Despite Ammiṣaduqa being assigned 21 years in the king lists, Richardson 2002, 200–206 proposed that Ammiṣaduqa should only be assigned 19 years, with Aṣ 17+e = Aṣ 5, Aṣ 17+b = Aṣ 18, and Aṣ 17+d = Aṣ 19. This would put the end of Samsuditana's reign in 1597 B.C. as opposed to 1595 B.C. of the standard Middle Chronology or the 1499 B.C. of the New Chronology, in Gasche et al. 1998.

25 For a more detailed breakdown of textual genres within the corpus, see Charpin 2020, 156.

26 CUSAS 29 41.

27 CUSAS 29 2 (Ae 14/iv/2); CUSAS 29 25 (Ae 21/xii/22); CUSAS 29 33 (Ad 1/xi/6); CUSAS 29 40 (Ae 21/vii/10), respectively.

28 Cf. Béranger 2019, nos. 1–3, specifically mentioning Zibbat-nārim, Dūr-šarrim, and Yankaḫu.

against the city of Nippur and the Ekur temple by an unnamed enemy in Ad 11, roughly 40 years after the city's conquest by the First Sealand Dynasty.[29]

Beyond evidence for the continued control of the region by Babylon, records of the performance of extispicies and the dossier of Enlil-mansum shed light on the cult of Nippur during this period as well. Several of these documents specifically record extispicies regarding travel from Dūr-Abiešuḫ to Nippur for the performance of sacrifices.[30]

The dossier of Enlil-mansum—the *nešakkum*-priest—is far more enlightening, however, as textual evidence suggests that he oversaw the Ekur temple.[31] Enlil-mansum first appears in the Dūr-Abiešuḫ corpus in Aṣ 5,[32] where he is heavily engaged in both economic and cult activities.[33] Within this dossier are several texts which mention sheep delivered for the daily offering of the Nippur cult. The earliest two of these texts—dated to Aṣ 8 and 9—mention that the sheep were bought specifically to Nippur.[34] A legal document within the corpus also mentions sacrifices performed in Nippur in Aṣ 2.[35] These documents demonstrate the continued cultic activity of the Nippur cult in its native city through the early years of Ammiṣaduqa. However, as discussed extensively by Charpin, the cult does relocate to the nearby Dūr-Abiešuḫ around this time.[36] This is seen in Enlil-mansum's later records of sheep delivered to Dūr-Abiešuḫ instead of Nippur.[37]

---

29 Following the translation of Charpin 2020, 157–158: "On the 19th of the 11th month, 500 mounted enemies and a troop of conscripts marched against Nippur. They entered the Ekur, the chariots […], the walls of the cella of [… were …] and they looted […]. [The …] were afraid; the riders, having made their juncture, left. On the 25th day of the 11th month, 300 mounted enemies entered the Ekur [(5-line gap)]. [In Nippur(?)] and Ekur, the enemy has been defeated (but) the enemy keeps (arriving) in Nippur daily."

30 Cf. CUSAS 29, 45 (Ad 11/ix/13): "3 UDU.ḪI.A *aš-šum* SIZKÚR / *a-na* EN.LÍL^{ki} *a-la-ki-im* / *a-di* U$_4$.20.KAM *i-pu-šu*," 3 sheep (total). Regarding: going to Nippur, until the 20th, (for) a sacrifice. They performed (the extispicies); 50 (Ad 12/vii/11); and 55 (Ad 12/viii/8).

31 See the discussion in Van Lerberghe and Voet 2009, 1–2.

32 CUSAS 8 2. A prosopographical study suggests it is possible that Enlil-mansum was in Dūr-Abiešuḫ before that date. This is due to his reference alongside a certain Utu-luti in CUSAS 8 23 and 24, who is also seen in CUSAS 8 54, alongside a group of *nešakkum* priests, which could include Enlil-mansum.

33 CUSAS 8 13, which records his participation in loans; CUSAS 8 23, a record of sheep delivered for the daily offering of the Nippur cult is received by Enlil-mansum.

34 CUSAS 8 23 and 24.

35 CUSAS 10 17.

36 Charpin 2020.

37 CUSAS 8 25–38.

4 Dating the Reconquest of Nippur

Until the publication of the first set of Dūr-Abiešuḫ tablets by Van Lerberghe and Voet (2009), no further conclusive evidence regarding the habitation of Central Babylonia following the capture of Nippur by the Sealand was known. This led to the general view that the region had been completely abandoned shortly after this conquest.[38] As discussed above, this view has now drastically changed. It can now conclusively be said that much of Central Babylonia was—once again—under the control of Babylon by the early years of Abiešuḫ's reign. This present section, then, shall pertain to the date in which the reconquest of Nippur—and possibly the rest of the region—occurred. In so doing, we will utilize contextual evidence from Dūr-Abiešuḫ, year names of Samsuiluna, and an analysis of a legal practice particular to Nippur—that of witnesses swearing upon Ninurta's Udbanuil weapon—to argue that the most likely year for this reconquest is Si 37.

The fortress of Dūr-Abiešuḫ—located at the outlet of the Ḫammurabi-nuḫuš-nišī canal—was situated only a few kilometers upstream of Nippur on the Euphrates River and formed part of a lengthy system of fortresses located on the Euphrates and Tigris rivers.[39] The military force of these southern fortresses was made up of both native Babylonians and large contingents of foreign mercenaries.[40]

The evidence within the Dūr-Abiešuḫ corpus demonstrates that far from being abandoned, the city of Nippur was both inhabited and still the site of many cultic activities.[41] Given the mention of rations for troops at Birti-Nippur and Dūr-Sinmuballiṭ (near Maškan-Šapir) in Ae 4,[42] the cities of Nippur and Maškan-Šapir must have been back under Babylonian control, even at this early stage. However, this raises a question. At what point did the Babylonians reconquer Nippur and the rest of the region?

Based on the textual record, Ilima-ilu controlled Nippur for at least two years, starting between the fourth and seventh months of Si 30, and lasting at least

38 See Charpin 2004, for an example of the understanding of this period before the publication of the present corpus.

39 Abraham and Van Lerberghe 2017, 6–7; Charpin 2020, 154–155; van Lerberghe and Voet 2016, 558–560 and Fig. 2.

40 Van Lerberghe and Voet 2016; van Koppen 2017; Charpin 2018; Thibaud 2021. These troops are often distinguished by their ethnicity (Kassites, Elamites, Gutians, and Sutaeans), or their place of origin (Elam, Ḫalaba, Arrapḫu, Gutûm, ldamaraz, Emutbalum, etc.). Cf. CUSAS 29 18, 22, 28, and 39; and CUSAS 29 5, 8, 32, 33, 39, and 40.

41 Discussed in section 3.

42 CUSAS 29 41.

until Si 31/viii/26.[43] This puts the reconquest of the region between the end of Si 31 and the beginning of Ae 4, a ten year period as Samsuiluna reigned for 38 years. This can be narrowed down further. An examination of the earliest Dūr-Abiešuḫ texts—from Ae 4—reveals no signs that the forts mentioned were under construction, or that there was any imminent military threat. Thus, it can be assumed that by Ae 4 this fortress—along with several other forts around Nippur and Maškan-Šapir—had already been in existence and under Babylonian control for several years. Given that Dūr-Abiešuḫ is named after Abiešuḫ, it should likewise be assumed that the fortress was constructed in the first couple of years of that king's reign, or at least finished in that time. It is also possible that the fortress was only renamed by Abiešuḫ since the site of Dūr-Abiešuḫ has not been found and dated. If this were the case, that event likely also would have transpired in the first few years of Abiešuḫ's reign, possibly immediately preceding its capture by the Babylonians. All of these indicate that Dūr-Abiešuḫ—and the region surrounding it—was under Babylonian control by the first few years of Abiešuḫ's reign. The terminus *post quem* for the reconquest of Nippur thus stands at the very end of Si 31 and the *ante quem* in the first couple of years of Abiešuḫ's reign.

What is left is to examine the textual records from this time in hopes of finding hints as to when Babylon was able to impose its dominance on the region. Unfortunately, as mentioned before, all text production disappears in this region during the intervening years, precisely the years under scrutiny. Yet, an event as massive as the conquest of Nippur and Central Babylonia should be expected to have created some form of textual trail.

5 The Nippur Cult in Babylon? Religious Evidence of Nippur's Reconquest.

One possible strand of evidence for the reconquest of Nippur can be found within the year names of Samsuiluna. Specifically, the year name Si 38, which reads: MU *sa-am-su-i-lu-na* LUGAL.E ^{d}U$_{4}$-BA-NU-ÍL-LA ŠITA KALA.GA ^{d}NIN-URTA UR-SAG GAL IN-NA-AN-GIBIL-A, "the year: Samsuiluna, the king, made anew the U[d]banuila, the mighty mace of Ninurta, the great hero."[44] Charpin (2004, 361, and see below) has stated that this would naturally imply the delivery of a divine gift to the Ekur temple in Nippur, where Nin-

43 This dating is based on BE 6/2 88.

44 Horsnell 1999, 231.

urta resided along with his father Enlil. If that were the case, it would indicate that Nippur was once again under the control of the Babylonian state at that time. However, that interpretation was not possible under the previous historical reconstruction in which Nippur had fallen into the hands of the Sealand Dynasty and subsequently been abandoned. As a result, it was necessary to assume that this year name was in reference to a location other than Nippur and that a transfer of the Nippur cult to another location had occured. Therefore, any use of this year name for reconstructing a potential reconquest of Nippur must first deal with this supposed transfer.

Given the assumed abandonment of Nippur, it had previously been proposed that the entirety of the Nippur cult had been transferred to Babylon, similar to the cults of Uruk and Larsa which had likewise moved to northern cities.[45] In discussing a possible transfer of the Nippur cult to Babylon, Pientka (1998) mentions two main sources of evidence. The first is the giving of votive gifts to the Enamtila temple in Babylon, as mentioned explicitly in the year names Ad 15, 19, 28, 31, and 34; Aṣ 5, 8, and 14.[46] A possible oblique reference is also seen in Sd 8. The second source of evidence are 'Enlil' or 'Ninurta' personal names recorded in Northern Babylonia.[47] It is important to note, however, that in this discussion Pientka herself suggests that the evidence in favor of a transfer of the cult to Babylon was not conclusive and that it was possible that both Nippur and the Ekur temple were not completely abandoned at that time.[48]

Despite the hesitancy of Pientka, the assumption that the Nippur cult must have transferred to Babylon continued. Thus, in response to the year name of Si 38, Charpin (2004, 361) states:

> *En principe, ces symboles divins étaient déposés à Nippur, non dans le temple de Ninurta, mais dans celui d'Enlil, l'Ekur: mais le fait qu'en l'an 37 Samsu-iluna fit exécuter un tel travail laisserait croire que les cultes de Nippur avaient pu être transférés en Babylonie du nord.*[49]

45 Van Lerberghe 2008, 127–128; George 2009, 137–138. Regarding the transfer of the cult from Uruk to Kiš and Dilbat, see Charpin 2004, 343. Pientka 1998, 179–189 placed this transition in Si 10 and suggested it is possible that the cult of Lagaš was also relocated to Kiš. Regarding the transfer of the Larsa cult to Babylon, see Charpin 2004, 343–345.

46 For details of the temple, see George 1992, 325–326; id. 1993, 130–131, no. 849.

47 Pientka 1998, 177–195.

48 Pientka 1998, 190–195.

49 Upon the publication of the Dūr-Abiešuḫ corpus, Charpin (2020, 156, n. 41) partly retracted this position, saying that "(*l*)*e nom de l'an 38 de Samsu-iluna, qui commémore la rénovation de l'arme du dieu Ninurta* (*nommée Ubanuil*), *pose un problème, dans la mesure où l'endrout où cette arme divine était conservée n'est pas mentionné*."

Even with knowledge of the Dūr-Abiešuḫ corpus and Nippur's continued cultic position, George later echoed Charpin's words, stating that surely this year name was to mark the relocation of the Nippur cult to Babylon, especially given an increase in mentions of kings bringing gifts to Enlil's Enamtila temple in Babylon in later Babylonian year names.[50]

However, the later popularity of the Enamtila should not be taken as an indication of the cult's transfer, given that this temple is first patronized by Hammurāpi, long before the supposed abandonment of Nippur.[51] Furthermore, the increase in patronization of the Enamtila does not begin until Ad 15, half a century after the supposed transfer.[52] Therefore, the patronization of the Enamtila by later kings of this period cannot be taken as evidence that the Enamtila was the only location in which Ninurta was patronized by the court. Instead in the words of Pientka (1998, 194), "*Vor allem Enlil wurde im offiziellen Kult der Hauptstadt Babylon die Verehrung zuteil, die ihm als sumerischem Reichsgott gebührte.*"

Similarly, while the study of Pientka does mention twelve names with the theophoric element 'Enlil' and sixteen names with the theophoric element 'Ninurta' born by individuals across all of Northern Babylon during the Late Old Babylonian Period, that number is still less than the number of names containing the element 'Nanāya' that Pientka identifies from just the city of Kiš alone, over the same time.

Finally, it is critical to note that before the publication of the Dūr-Abiešuḫ corpus—except for a handful of personal names and year names[53]—only one reference to the gods of Nippur in the Late Old Babylonian Period was known.[54]

---

50 George 2009, 137.

51 RIME 4 3.6.3 mentions Hammurāpi building a storehouse for Enlil in Babylon; the colophon explicitly mentions the Enamtila. Hammurāpi (Hi) 18 also mentions the provision of a dais for Enlil in Babylon, almost certainly another oblique reference to the Enamtila.

52 Gabbay and Boivin (2018, 37) have rightfully suggested that the drastic increase in mentions of the patronization of the Enamtila likely indicates a weakening of Nippur's cultic role in the Babylonian state. However, this should not be seen as evidence of a cultic transfer. Instead, it needs to be noted that only a few years before Ad 15, there had been a large-scale invasion of Nippur, in which the Ekur itself was damaged; CUSAS 29 205. Thus, instead of seeing this as evidence of a transfer of the cult to Babylon, it should be seen as indicative of the intense conflict occurring in Central Babylonia at that time, as well as the damaged nature of the temple itself. Charpin 2020, 164 has even suggested that this conflict and damage could have been the cause of the eventual transfer to the more defensible, nearby fortress.

53 Cf. the year name of Aṣ 17+e.

54 CUSAS 8 3; Pientka 1998, 193.

The reference, which is found in an undated letter from Sippar-Yaḫrurum, invokes the gods Enlil, Ninlil, Ninurta, and Nusku.[55] However, it also explicitly mentions a boat trip to Dūr-Abiešuḫ. With the discovery of our corpus, it is now possible to understand this letter in the context of Dūr-Abiešuḫ. Thus, instead of assuming it indicated the presence of the Nippur cult in Northern Babylon, it is now possible—and more likely—that the sender of the letter was originally from the area of Nippur.

Due to the previous lack of evidence for persistent habitation of Nippur during this period, it was natural to assume that the cult of Nippur followed the same pattern as many of the other southern cults: relocating to Northern Babylonia. This argument was, however, predominantly an argument from silence, with only limited evidence, as Pientka herself pointed out.[56] The Dūr-Abiešuḫ corpus, however, allows—for the first time—making an argument from extensive evidence. To wit, as discussed above, the corpus demonstrates that not only was Nippur not abandoned in the years following its conquest by the First Sealand Dynasty, but within a short time it was once again under the control of Babylon and cultic activities were once again taking place in the region. This in turn has caused Charpin to drastically modify his earlier historical reconstruction. Instead, Charpin (2020) argues the cult remained in Nippur until the early years of Ammiṣaduqa's reign. At that time it was relocated to the nearby Dūr-Abiešuḫ.[57] Yet, even if it is unlikely that the year name of Si 38 refers to the Enamtila, what evidence is there that it should be explicitly connected to the Ekur?

In discussing the evidence for connecting this year name to the Ekur, and thereby Nippur, the mention of Ninurta's Udbanuil weapon takes center stage. This weapon is frequently connected directly to legal proceedings within the city of Nippur. This can be demonstrated by three Old Babylonian legal documents from Nippur, which record a legal practice specific to that city, the practice of witnesses swearing upon Ninurta's Udbanuil weapon.

The first document, which records a land dispute, mentions that both parties, along with witnesses, were made to speak in front of the Udbanuil.[58] The

55 AbB 7 118; Pientka 1998, 193.

56 Pientka 1998, 190–195.

57 Charpin 2020. Some cultic officials may have moved north following the conquest of Nippur, which could explain the presence of Taqîš-Gula in Babylon. However, this move would have been very short-lived as the evidence for the cult being in Babylon is practically negligible.

58 BE 6/2 49:28–32: DI.KU$_5$.MEŠ *ši-bu-ú-us-sú-nu* / *ma-har* ^{d}UD.BA.NU.ÍL *qá-ba-a-am iq-bu-ú-šu-nu-ši* / *šu-mu-um-li-ib-ši i-na mi-it-gur-ti-šu* / LÚ.KI.INIM.MA.MEŠ *a-na* ^{d}UD.BA.NU.ÍL / *ú-ul ú-sa-an-na-aq-šu-nu-ti iq-bi-ma*, "*Les juges leur ordonnèrent de donner leur*

second document, which concerns the paternity of a man in an inheritance dispute, likewise references the use of Udbanuil in oath-taking, as well as the weapon acting as a witness to the writing up of a legal document.[59] The third document, a model court case, yet again mentions that both parties of the dispute are made to stand in front of the Udbanuil.[60]

The Dūr-Abiešuḫ corpus adds additional evidence from yet another legal document. The document, which is extant in three copies and dates to Sd 5, records an inheritance dispute over the prebend of *pāšišum* priests of Ninurta.[61] Near the end of the record, it states that "at that time the aforesaid Gimil-Marduk lifted the standard (^{giš}tukul) of Ninurta in the presence of (a list of dignitaries). The witnesses gave their testimony before Ninurta, the god of their city."[62]

Although this text does not explicitly name the 'the standard of Ninurta,' the similarities between this scene and those mentioned in the preceding cases point to the conclusion that this standard and the Udbanuil are the same. Despite this event taking place outside of Nippur, the list of dignitaries connects it with the Nippur cult and the Ekur. Of special mention is the presence of Enlil-mansum, the *nešakkum*-priest and overseer of the Ekur.[63]

Although the act of taking oaths in front of various divine symbols was common in the Old Babylonian Period, the use of the Udbanuil was unique to Nippur, due assuredly to its association with Ninurta.[64] Richardson (2021) goes so far as to suggest that the Udbanuil mentioned in these legal texts is the exact same one mentioned in Si 38.[65] It is noteworthy that the first two legal texts mentioned date to Si 19 and Si 26, immediately before Nippur's conquest by

---

témoignage par devant Udbanuil. Mais Šumum-libši de son plein gré dit: 'Je ne veux pas soumettre les témoins à Udbanuil.'"; Charpin 2019b, 45.

59 Leichty 1989 = PBS 5 100.

60 Klein and Sharlach 2007, CBS 11324. ii: 13–17: UB.ŠU.UKKIN.⸢NA?⸣ / ^{d}UD.BA.NU.[ÍL.LA] / ⸢IN⸣.GUB.B[U.UŠ] / ⸢LÚ⸣ KI.IN[IM.MA.BI] / IM.TA.È.E.[EŠ], "*Ils se sont tenus dans* (*la cour*) *Ubšu-ukkina devant* (*l'arme*) *Udbanuila. Les témoins ont été produits: ils ont confirmé que* (*etc.*)."; Charpin 2019b, 45.

61 CUSAS 10 17. George 2009, 142–148 claims that the document is a model court composition. Charpin 2019a; id. 2020, 166–168 and 179–180, however, argues that it should be seen as a genuine record. This argument is beyond the scope of the present study; suffice it to say the present author sides with Charpin.

62 CUSAS 10 17: 73–80.

63 CUSAS 10 17: 85. For a discussion of Enlil-mansum, see above, p. 42, as well as Van Lerberghe and Voet 2009, 1–2.

64 The use of his weapon then, as a pseudo-stand in—whether intentional or not—is a quite logical corollary. See George 2009, 151–152 with previous lit.

65 Richardson 2021, 31.

the First Sealand Dynasty.[66] Meanwhile, the legal document from Dūr-Abiešuḫ dates from Sd 5. As recently argued by Charpin (2020), this was only shortly before this time that the cult of Nippur had been relocated to Dūr-Abiešuḫ from Nippur, and not from Babylon. Thus, even at this point, the cult and judicial organization were still in the practice of using the Udbanuil for legal proceedings. Thus, this explicit use of the Udbanuil was certainly contemporary with the year name of Si 38, having appeared shortly before and again only a few generations later.

Given the evidence in favor of the continued presence of the cult of Nippur in its traditional home, the persistent connection of the Udbanuil with the cult and judicial organization of Nippur before and after the conquest of the city by the Sealand, and the general lack of strong evidence for a transition of the cult to Babylon, the previous view that "[t]he removal of major Nippurian cults to the capital was surely the occasion of Samsuiluna's restoration of Ninurta's weapon Udbanuilla,"[67] can no longer be supported. In examining the record of a votive gift by Samsuiluna of a restored Udbanuil, it appears far more likely that this gift would be delivered to Nippur and not to Babylon. In other words, the most plausible understanding of the year name of Si 38 is that Nippur must have been under Babylonian control at the time of the votive gift.

It is possible that the rededicating of the Udbanuil did not occur immediately following this reconquest, but only some years afterward. However, given the importance of the weapon in legal proceedings of the city, a statement regarding its restoration would serve well as the marker of Nippur's reconquest by the Babylonian crown. Similarly, given the esteemed position of Nippur in Mesopotamia, it should be expected that such an event would be accompanied by fanfare and propaganda as is seen in several of Samsuiluna's earlier year names.[68] Although the reconquest of Nippur and the dedication of the Udbanuil are not explicitly connected, the dedication's temporal relation to the period in which we would expect just such a statement is far too striking to be treated as a mere coincidence.

Therefore, until much more explicit information is provided, it should be the working hypothesis within the reconstruction of this period that Si 37—seven years after the city's capture by the Sealand—should be seen as the date of the Nippur's reconquest. This would leave only a year between this event and the ascension to the throne of Abiešuḫ, which fits in very well with Boivin's (2018,

66 BE 6/2 49 and PBS 5 100, respectively.

67 CUSAS 10 137.

68 Cf. Si 10, 11, and 12.

99) observation that "(t)he construction of that fortress [Dūr-Abiešuḫ], probably in the very first years of Abī-ešuḫ's reign, must have followed immediately the recapture of Nippur from Sealand I control and been part of Babylon's strategy to defend it."

6 Conclusion

The publication of the Dūr-Abiešuḫ corpus has answered many questions that had surrounded Central Babylonia during the Late Old Babylonian Period, a period poorly understood previously. This article has sought to continue that trend by proposing the date for the reconquest of Nippur from the Sealand Dynasty should be placed in Samsuiluna's 37th year. This suggestion is supported by the mention of the rededication of Ninurta's Udbanuil weapon in the year name of Si 38. Although this event had previously not been connected to Nippur—due to the belief that the city had been abandoned—the Dūr-Abiešuḫ corpus, legal documents, and a lack of evidence for a transition of the Nippur cult to the north have allowed us to connect these two events and thereby notice the relationship between this rededication and the reconquest of the city.

Excursus—Publication History of the Dūr-Abiešuḫ Corpus

It is worth briefly explaining my listing of 310 Dūr-Abiešuḫ texts, as this number does not perfectly match those listed by others; see table 1. For example, Charpin (2020, 155–156) only lists 296. Part of this discrepancy is in that he counts CUSAS 10 17 as one text, despite it consisting of three duplicates. Additionally, it seems that he does not include CUSAS 18 3, 13, or 14, although he does not explicitly mention this. He also (id., 189) suggests that CUSAS 29 2 likely did not originate in Dūr-Abiešuḫ either, as it deals with grain at Kār-Nabium. Finally, he also (id., 185) doubts the origins of CUSAS 29 118–124. This leaves a two-tablet discrepancy between the count of Charpin 2020 and that of this study.

ARCHIBAB similarly counts fewer Dūr-Abiešuḫ texts than the present study. Charpin might very well be correct, in that several texts are erroneously seen as originating from Dūr-Abiešuḫ. However, until a fuller analysis of this topic is carried out, it is too early to rule out that these texts could have been created at—or brought to—Dūr-Abiešuḫ, even if the locations they deal with are not the fortress itself.

TABLE 1 Publication history of the Dūr-Abiešuḫ corpus

Publication	Texts
George 2009	4 (nos. 16, 17a–c)
Van Lerberghe and Voet 2009	89
George 2013	4 (nos. 3, 4, 13, 14)
Földi 2014	1
Abraham and Van Lerberghe 2017	206
Feliu 2017	1 (no. 7)
Földi 2017	1
Sigrist, Gabbay, and Avila 2017	1 (no. 5)
Béranger 2019	3
Total	310

References

Abraham, Kathleen, and Karel van Lerberghe. 2017. *A Late Old Babylonian Temple Archive from Dur-Abieshuh: The Sequel.* CUSAS 29. Bethesda: CDL.

Armstrong, Jack A., and Margaret C. Brandt. 1994. "Ancient Dunes at Nippur." In *Cinquante-deux reflexions sur le Proche-Orient ancien offertes en homage à Leon De Meyer.* MHEM 2, edited by Hermann Gasche, 255–263. Leuven: Peeters.

Béranger, Marine. 2019. "Dur-Abi-Ešuh and the Aftermath of the Attack on Nippur: New Evidence from Three Unpublished Letters." *RA* 113: 99–122.

Béranger, Marine. 2022. "A Late Old Babylonian List of Rations from Dur-Abi-ešuh in the Cotsen collection (Los Angeles)." *NABU* 2022: 123–127.

Boivin, Odette. 2018. *The First Dynasty of the Sealand in Mesopotamia.* SANER 20. Boston: De Gruyter.

Charpin, Dominique and Antoine Jacquet. ARCHIBAB. http://www.archibab.fr/.

Charpin, Dominique. 1999–2000. "Review: Die spätaltbabylonische Zeit: Abiešuḫ bis Samsuditana. Quellen, Jahresdaten, Geschichte, (= Imgula 2), by Rosel Pientka." *AfO* 46–47: 322–324.

Charpin, Dominique. 2004. "Histoire politique du Proche-Orient amorrite (2002–1595)." In *Mesopotamien: Die altbabylonische Zeit.* OBO 160, edited by Dominique Charpin, Dietz Edzard, and Marten Stol, 25–384. Fribourg and Göttingen: Academic Press Fribourg.

Charpin, Dominique. 2015. "Six nouveaux recueils de documents paleo-babyloniens." *RA* 109: 143–196.

Charpin, Dominique. 2018. "À l'occasion des dix ans du projet ARCHIBAB." *RA* 112: 177–208.

Charpin, Dominique. 2019a. "En marge d'EcritUr, 6: CUSAS 10 17 et l'onomastique théophore de Dumununna." *NABU* 2019: 77–78.

Charpin, Dominique. 2019b. "Les symboles divins dans les archives paléo-babyloniennes." In *Représenter dieux et hommes dans le Proche-Orient ancien et dans la Bible*, edited by Thomas Römer, Hervé Gonzalez, and Lionel Marti, 38–51. Leuven: Peeters.

Charpin, Dominique. 2020. "Un clergé en exil: le transfert des Dieux de Nippur à Dur-Abi-ešuh." In *Des Polythéismes aux monothéismes: Mélanges d'assyriologie offerts à Marcel Sigrist*, edited by Uri Gabbay and Jean Jacques Pérennès, 149–187. Leuven: Peeters.

Dalley, Stephanie. 2009. *Babylonian Tablets from the First Sealand Dynasty in the Schøyen Collection.* CUSAS 9. Bethesda: CDL.

Feliu, Lluis. 2017. "Cuneiform Texts from the Campalans Collection." *AuOr* 35: 85–96.

Földi, Zsombor. 2017. "Cuneiform Tablets and the Antiquities Market: The Archives from Dūr-Abī-ešuḫ." *Distant Worlds Journal* 2: 7–27.

Földi, Zsombor. 2014. "Cuneiform Texts in the Kunsthistorisches Museum Wien, Part IV: A New Text from Dūr-Abī-ēšuḫ." *WZKM* 104: 31–55.

Frayne, Douglas. 1990. *Old Babylonian Period (2003–1595 BC).* RIME 4. Toronto: University of Toronto.

Gasche, Herman, Jack A. Armstrong, Steven W. Cole, and Vahagn G. Gurzaydan. 1998. *Dating the Fall of Babylon: A Reappraisal of Second-Millennium Chronology.* MHEM 4. Ghent: The University of Ghent and the Oriental Institute of the University of Chicago.

George, Andrew. 1992. *Babylonian Topographical Texts.* OLA 40. Leuven: Peeters.

George, Andrew. 1993. *House Most High: The Temples of Ancient Mesopotamia.* MC 5. Winona Lake: Eisenbrauns.

George, Andrew. 2009. *Babylonian Literary Texts in the Schøyen Collection.* CUSAS 10. Bethesda: CDL.

George, Andrew. 2013. *Babylonian Divinatory Texts Chiefly in the Schøyen Collection.* CUSAS 18. Bethesda: CDL.

Gibson, McGuire. 1992. "Patterns of Occupation at Nippur." In *Nippur at the Centennial. Papers Read at the 35e Rencontre Assyriologique Internationale, Philadelphia, 1988.* Occasional Publications of the Samuel Noah Kramer Fund 14, edited by Maria de Jong Ellis, 33–54. Philadelphia: Philadelphia University.

Goddeeris, Anne. 2016. *The Old Babylonian Administrative Texts in the Hilprecht Collection Jena.* Vol. 1. TMH 10. Wiesbaden: Harrassowitz.

Horsnell, Malcolm J. 1999. *The Year-Names of the First Dynasty of Babylon.* Vol. 2. Hamilton: McMaster University.

Klein, Jacob, and Tonia M. Sharlach. 2007. "A Collection of Model Court Cases from Old Babylonian Nippur (CBS 11324)." *ZA* 97: 1–25.

Leichty, Erle. 1989. "Feet of Clay." In *DUMU-E$_2$-DUB-BA-A: Studies in Honor of Åke W. Sjöberg*, edited by Hermann Behrens, Darlene Loding, and Martha T. Roth, 349–356. Philadelphia: The University Museum.

Pientka, Rosel. 1998. *Die spätbabylonische Zeit: Abiešuḫ bis Samsuditana: Quellen, Jahresdaten, Geschichte*, Teil 1. Munster: Rhema.

Richardson, Seth. 2002. "The Collapse of a Complex State: A Reappraisal of the End of the First Dynasty of Babylon, 1683–1597 B.C." PhD diss., Columbia University.

Richardson, Seth. 2021. "Place and Portability: Divine Emblems in Old Babylonian Law." In *As Above, So Below: Religion and Geography—Proceedings following a Workshop Conducted during the 62nd Rencontre Assyriologique Internationale*, edited by Shana Zaia and Gina Konstantopolous, 28–73. Winona Lake, IN: Eisenbrauns.

Roth, Martha T. 1983. "The Slave and the Scoundrel. CBS 10467, A Sumerian Morality Tale?" *JAOS* 103: 275–282.

Roth, Martha T. 1998. "Gender and Law: A Case Study from Ancient Mesopotamia." In *Gender and Law in the Hebrew Bible and the Ancient Near East*, edited by Victor H. Matthews, 173–184. London: Bloomsbury.

Sigrist, Marcel, Uri Gabbay, and Mark Avila. 2017. "Cuneiform Tablets and Other Inscribed Objects from Collections in Jerusalem." In *The First Ninety Years: A Sumerian Celebration in Honor of Miguel Civil*, edited by Lluis Feliu, Fumi Karahashu, and Gonzalo Rubio, 311–336. Berlin—Boston: De Gruyter.

Stone, Elizabeth. 1977. "Economic Crisis and Social Upheaval in Old Babylonian Nippur." In *Mountains and Lowlands: Essays in the Archaeology of Greater Mesopotamia*. Bibliotheca Mesopotamica 7, edited by Louis D. Levin and Theodore Young, 267–289. Malibu: Undena.

Stone, Elizabeth. 1987. *Nippur Neighborhoods*. SAOC 44. Chicago: The Oriental Institute.

Thibaud, Nicolas. 2021. "Samsu-iluna, les mercenaires kassites et la mesure de Marduk: la métrologie au service de l'histoire politique." *NABU* 2021: 168–170.

Van Lerberghe, Karel. 2008. "The Clergy and Religious Institutions of Nippur in the Late Old-Babylonian Period." In *Studies in Ancient Near Eastern World View and Society: Presented to Marten Stol*, edited by Robartus J. van der Spek, 127–131. Bethesda: CDL.

Van Lerberghe, Karel, and Gabriella Voet. 2009. *A Late Old Babylonian Temple Archive from Dur-Abieshuh*. CUSAS 8. Bethesda: CDL.

Van Lerberghe, Karel, and Gabriella Voet. 2010. "Kassite Mercenaries at Abiešuḫ's Fortress." In: *Why Should Someone who Knows Something Conceal it? Cuneiform Studies in Honor of David I. Owen on his 70th Birthday*, edited by Alexandera Kleinerman and Jack. M. Sasson, 181–187. Bethesda: CDL.

Van Lerberghe, Karel, and Gabriella Voet. 2016. "Dūr-Abiešuḫ and Venice Settlements In-between Great Rivers." In *Libiamo Ne'lieti Calici: Ancient Near Eastern Studies Presented to Lucio Milano on the Occasion of his 65th Birthday by Pupils, Colleagues, and Friends*, edited by Paola Coro, 557–563. Munster: Ugarit Verlag.

Zomer, Elyza. 2019. *Middle Babylonian Literary Texts from the Frau Professor Hilprecht Collection, Jena*. TMH 12. Wiesbaden: Harrassowitz.

CHAPTER 3

The Statue of Idrimi and the Term *mānaḫtu/mānaḫātu*

Yoram Cohen | ORCID: 0000-0001-8492-1330
Tel Aviv University
ycohen1@tauex.tau.ac.il

Abstract

The purpose of this article is to discuss the word *mānaḫtu/mānaḫātu* which appears four times in the Statue of Idrimi inscription. The exact meaning of the word is not evident. Evidence from the *Maison d'Urtenu* from Ugarit will help us assess the meaning of the word in the inscription. A short discussion of the historical significance of the term in Idrimi's Alalakh under the hegemony of the Mittanian state will close our contribution.

Keywords

Statue of Idrimi – Alalakh – Mitanni – Ugarit – Taxation

תקציר

מטרת המאמר לדון במילה *mānaḫtu/mānaḫātu*, אשר מופיעה ארבע פעמים בכתובת של הפסל של אידרימי. המשמעות המדוייקת של המילה איננה ברורה דיה. עדות מהארכיון של אורתנו מן העיר אוגרית מסייעת בידינו לקבוע את משמעות המילה בכתובת. לאור זאת, נסכם בדיון את המשמעות ההיסטורית של המילה בזמנו של המלך אידרימי בעיר אללח׳ תחת השלטון של ממלכת מיתני.

מילות מפתח

הפסל של אידרימי – אללח׳ – מיתני – אוגרית – מיסוי

 | DOI:10.1163/9789004526822_004

المستخلص

تستهدف هذه الدّراسة البحث في الكلمة *mānaḫtu/mānaḫātu* الّتي تظهر أربع مرّات في النّقش على تمثال إدريمي. المعنى الدّقيق للكلمة غير واضح تماما. الموادّ من أرشيف أورتينو في مدينة أوغاريت تساعدنا على فهم معنى الكلمة في النّقش. في نهاية المقال نبحث في الأهمّيّة التّاريخيّة لهذا المصطلح في مدينة ألالاخ في عهد إدريمي تحت سيطرة مملكة ميتاني.

الكلمات المفتاحيّة

تمثال إدريمي – ألالاخ – ميتاني – أوغاريت – الضّرائب

Since its publication in 1949 by Sidney Smith, the inscription of the Statue of Idrimi has benefited from multiple studies, some at book length.[1] Discussions concentrated on the inscription's script, language, literary genre, and historical content. Recently, it has benefited from a concise and useful online edition by Lauinger (2021), named as *The Electronic Idrimi*. Still, not all problems are solved and there are even difficulties in understanding the proper meaning of some words and expressions. The purpose of this article is to discuss the word *mānaḫtu/mānaḫātu* which appears four times and at two different passages, and whose exact meaning is not evident. Evidence from the *Maison d'Urtenu* from Ugarit will help us assess the meaning of the word in the inscription. A short discussion of the historical significance of the term in Idrimi's Alalakh under the hegemony of the Mittanian state will close our contribution.

The words *mānaḫtu* (Sg.) and *mānaḫātu* (Pl.) appear four times in Idrimi's inscription: *ma-na-ḫ*[*a-t*]*e*-ḪÉ (l. 47), *ma-na-ḫa-te*$^{\text{hi.a}}$ (l. 51), *ma-na-ḫa-te*^{meš} (l. 54), all in the plural form, and only once in the singular *ma-na-aḫ-ti-ia* (l. 103). This is of significane as will be discussed later.

The appearance of the term *mānaḫātu* (Pl.) in lines 47, 51, and 54 is within the context of the relationship of Idrimi with the Hurrian king Parrattarna. The singular form appears at line 103, towards the close of the inscription, at its summary. Let us start with l. 103, which, together with l. 104, read as follows.

---

1 This paper is part of the project *Forging an Empire: Hittite Imperial Administration from the Mediterranean to the Euphrates*, funded by the Gerda Henkel Foundation.

ma-na-aḫ-ti-ia a-na ⸢ugu⸣*-ia aš-ṭú-ur li-*⸢*dá-na*⸣*-gal-šu-nu ù a-na* ugu*-ia li-ik-ta-na-ra-bu*

The meaning of ll. 103–104 is clear, and the word *mānaḫtu* presents no translation problem. Idrimi sums up his achievements by stating that he wrote about his *mānaḫtu*, which can be translated as hardship, trouble, or even adventure, so that people would read about it and provide him with their blessing.[2] The use of *mānaḫtu* in this sense can be found in other instances, many brought by CAD/M1: 203, under 1. 'toil, misery, weariness'.[3]

The earlier appearances in the inscription of *mānaḫātu*, this time in the plural, are more difficult to explain, when it is certain that they do not convey the same meaning of *mānaḫtu* of line 103, unless taken in their very literal (and meaningless) sense.[4] They appear in a passage which speaks about Idrimi's and his forefathers' relationship with the Hurrian overlords. Idrimi states that the Hurrian king Parrattarna was hostile to him for seven years, but at (the end of) the seventh year, Idrimi wrote to the king in order to renew his pact with the Hurrians. Here is the passage in question (ll. 46–55), with Idrimi as the speaker.

46. … *ad-bu-ub*
47. *ma-na-ḫa-*[*te*]-ḪÉ *ša a-bu-te*$^{\text{ḫi.a}}$*-ia i-nu-ma*
48. *a-bu-te*$^{\text{ḫi.a}}$*-ia a-na* ugu*-šu-nu in-na-ḫu-ú*
49. *ù* [*a*]*-wa-ti-ni a-na* lugal$^{\text{ḫi.a}}$ *ša* érin.meš *Ḫur-ri*^{ki} *da-mi-iq*
50. ⸢*ù*⸣ *a-*⸢*na*⸣ *bi-ri-šu-nu* nam.érin *dan-na*
51. ⸢*iš*⸣*-ku-nu-ni*$_7$*-na* lugal *dan-nu ma-na-ḫa-te*$^{\text{ḫi.a}}$
52. *ša pa-nu-ti-ni ù* nam.érin *ša bi-ri-šu-nu iš-me*$^{!}$*-ma*
53. *ù á-ti ma-mi-ti ip-ta-la-aḫ aš-šum a-wa-at*
54. *ma-mi-ti ù aš-šum ma-na-ḫa-te*^{meš}*-ni šu-ul-mi-ia*
55. *im-tá-ḫar*

---

2 We read here with Lauinger 2021, n. 80, ⸢ugu⸣*-ia*. Dietrich and Loretz 1981, 207 and 230, read dub*-ia*, 'my tablet', which is followed by Durand 2011, 150. Another suggestion is to read the sign as alam*-ia*, 'statue', with Smith 1949, 22, and later by Oller 1977, 18 and 145, and Greenstein and Marcus 1976, 66 and 68, followed by Longman 2003, 480. Whatever reading is decided upon ('about myself', 'upon my tablet', or 'on my statue'), the meaning of *mānaḫtu* is the same.

3 Note that the comparison of l. 103 to SB Gilgameš, Tablet 1, l. 10, in order to claim that Idrimi's scribe was inspired by the Gilgameš text, as suggested by Greenstein and Marcus 1976, 81–82, is less obvious nowadays. The earlier reading [*irḫu*]*ṣ*, '[he engra]ved', was changed with [*ša-k*]*in*, '[he set d]own', giving us [*ša-k*]*in ina* $^{\text{na4}}$*narê*(na.rú.a) *ka-lu ma-na-aḫ-ti*, '[he set d]own on a stele all (his) labours'; George 2003, 538–539, 779; and confirmed by the Ugarit ms. However, the meaning of *mānaḫtu* in both instances is still very much the same, as its echo of Akkadian literature is probably deliberate, as argued by Lauinger 2021b, 29–32.

4 Greenstein and Marcus 1976, 81.

Various translations have tried to solve the meaning of the term *ma-na-ḫa-te* in the passage, which is essential for determining the nature of the relationship between Idrimi and the Hurrians. Some have opted for the more literal, basing their translation on the assumed shared root of *mānaḫātu* and *anāḫu* or *nâḫu* (either of which may stand behind the form *in-na-ḫu-ú*, by itself problematic; see below). Others have relied more on the context of the passage and its relation to the entire inscription. A few translations rendering *mānaḫātu* and then the verbal form *in-na-ḫu-ú* (l. 48) can be presented here.

Smith (1949, 17 and 104): 'terms of peace, treaty', and 'were at peace relations' (from the verb *nâḫu*).
Oppenheim (1969): 'services', and 'been in their (the kings') service'.[5]
Greenstein and Marcus (1976, 67 and 81–82), 'treaties', with 'were allied' (from *nâḫu*).
Oller (1977, 13 and 51–52): 'efforts', and 'labored'.
Borger (1979, 23): '*Anstrengungen*'.
Dietrich and Loretz (1981, 205, 215, 216–217): '*Bemühungen, Mühsal*', and '*verbrüdert hatten*' (from *aḫû* II, AHw: 22).
Durand (2011, 141[+148]): '*tribulations* (*à son service*)' and '*avaient fait un pacte de fraternité*' (from *aḫû* II, AHw: 22).
Longman 2003, 479[+3]: 'vassal service' and 'made a treaty'.
Lauinger 2021b, 24–25: 'service', and 'toiled'.

The most recent discussion of *mānaḫātu* is offered by Lauinger 2021b, who rightly saw its meaning as 'vassal service', and anaylzied it as a marker of Alalakh's political subordination to Mittani, although he refrained from being more precise regarding the practical meaning of the term.

Hence, after reviewing some of the translations of the term under discussion in passage, can we pin down a more precise meaning of *mānaḫātu* in this context, as well as the meaning of the form *in-na-ḫu-ú*? This is where the *Maison d'Urtenu* letters from Ugarit can help us.

The term *mānaḫātu* appears in several letters exchanged between the Hittite administration in Syria and the king of Ugarit, as well as the governor of the city. As can be concluded on the basis of the Ugarit letters, *mānaḫātu* means tribute or taxation delivered to Hittites by the kingdom of Ugarit.[6] That *mānaḫātu* in Ugarit means 'gift' or 'tribute' was already suspected by Albright (1957),

5 And also CAD/M/1 (1977): 206.
6 Lackenbacher and Malbran-Labat 2016, 48–49; Vita, 2021; Cohen and Torrecilla, Forthcoming.

who said that it is 'scarcely the plural of Accadian *mānaḫtu*, "toil" but is rather the plural of the noun which appears as *minḥah*, "gift, offerings", in Hebrew […].'[7] The same or close meaning can be attributed to the Ugaritic alphabetic rendering of the word, *mnh*(*t*). Attested to rather rarely, nonetheless, it is clear that it means 'gift' or 'tribute'.[8]

The *mānaḫātu* tribute is extracted in the form of grain staples, and, in cases where specified, in huge volumes. These were supplied upon demand, and not, as far as can be understood, according to a fixed term. A few examples will suffice to demonstrate the meaning of the word and its usage within the context of Hittite Syria.

The letter RSO 23 81 was sent by a Hittite official writing to Ugarit's governor. The official says (ll. 32–35), '[No]w, the tribute (*ma-na-ʾa-ti*) about which [you wr]ote me thus, "Behold, [I have] sent 10 *kurru* of wheat (GIG.MEŠ)." (However), the wheat which you sent me is (only) 9 *kurru* of wheat.'

Another letter, RSO 23 104, has another Hittite official writing to Niqmadu III, the king of Ugarit. He tells the king of Ugarit that (ll. 7–15), 'in the city of Magdal[a], (from) all the fields which were sown, your tribute (*ma-na-ḫa-te-k*[*a*]) should be collected and delivered. Now, I will not release (*ul umeššar*) the fields which were sown.' The sense of these lines is that the *mānaḫātu*, as grain cultivated at Magdala, will be delivered to the Hittites, and the fields in question will not be exempt from this obligation.

RSO 23 27 addressed to the king of Ugarit is from two Hittite officials acting on behalf of the Hittite king himself at Hattuša. They demand that (ll. 7–15) Ugarit supply 3,000 units (*sūtu*?) of tribute (*ma-na-ḫa-ti*), one can safely assume, as grain staples, as is demanded by His Majesty, that is, the Hittite king himself at Ḫattuša. Even though it is not detailed, the unit implied is probably the *sūtu*, given the high number. The weight of the *mānaḫātu* then would have been a staggering 18.6 tons, at least.

To conclude, it is clear that the *mānaḫātu* were a kind of vassal tribute or taxation. Once Ugarit had delivered the *mānaḫātu*, as grain staples, the Hittites directed the grain staples wherever they were needed. Towns in the Ugarit-Mukiš border were instrumental in producing and/or distributing the grain staples.

Such tax stipulations in Hittite Syria does not mean that they were exercised in Mitanni dominated Alalakh or Halab. However, there is enough to suppose that this was the case, even if the details may have been different. To begin

7 The Hebrew מִנְחָה can mean 'offerings', but in political contexts, it means tribute; cf. Judges 3:15; Sam 2, 8:6.

8 Del Olmo Lete and Sanmartín 2015, 556; Vita, 2021.

with, one can certainly compare the political set-up. Ugarit and Hatti held a vassal and overlord relationship as much as Alalakh/Halab and Mitanni did. Furthermore, the geo-political context in Mitanni Syria can be considered. We are aware of the Hurrians extracting tribute or levies at Alalakh itself.[9] At Azû there is evidence of the collection of some tribute or tax.[10] And at Emar the so-called Arana-documents stand witness to the tribute delivered to the Hurrians.[11] More specifically, the very term itself appears in a well-studied document from Emar, Gs-Kutscher 6. The document is a land-grant provided by the king of Emar to a certain Irib-Baʿal as a gift for redeeming the tribute of four daughters of the king in addition to gold imposed on Emar by the Hurrian King (lugal kur *ḫur-ri*). It is said that Irib-Baʿal, ***ma-na-aḫ-ta*** gal *liṭ-ṭi* uru-*lì-šu ù be-li-šu e-te-pu-uš* (ll. 16–18), which is to be translated as 'had paid the heavy tribute of the hostages of his city and his lord'. This demonstrates that the meaning of *mān-aḫtu* as 'tribute' in a political context can certainly be implied. In short, because the context of the passage and the geo-historical circumstances in Syria there is nothing that stands in our way of understanding *mānaḫātu* in the Idrimi inscription as tribute or taxes of some sort, although not necessarily cereals. When this translation of the term is taken into consideration, the difficulties of meaning of the verb *in-na-ḫu-ú* can be resolved.

Hereby follows the passage, arranged according to its proper sentences (and not as arranged across the statue's surface), and my translation:

> (*adbub*) *ma-na-ḫa-*[*te*]-ḪÉ [a] *ša a-bu-te*$^{\text{ḫi.a}}$*-ia*
> *i-nu-ma a-bu-te*$^{\text{ḫi.a}}$*-ia a-na* ugu-*šu-nu in-na-ḫu-ú* [b]
> *ù* [*a*]*-wa-ti-ni a-na* lugal$^{\text{ḫi.a}}$ *ša* érin.meš *Ḫur-ri*^{ki} *da-mi-iq*
> ⌜*ù*⌝ *a-* ⌜*na*⌝ *bi-ri-šu-nu* nam.érin *dan-na* ⌜*iš*⌝*-ku-nu-*ni_7*-na*
> lugal *dan-nu ma-na-ḫa-te*$^{\text{ḫi.a}}$ *ša pa-nu-ti-ni ù* nam.érin *ša bi-ri-šu-nu*
> *iš-me*$^{!}$*-ma*
> *ù it-ti* [c] *ma-mi-ti ip-ta-la-aḫ*
> *aš-šum a-wa-at ma-mi-ti ù aš-šum ma-na-ḫa-te*^{meš}*-ni šu-ul-mi-ia*
> *im-tá-ḫar*

… (And I spoke about) the tribute of my forefathers: "When my forefathers bore (the tribute) upon themselves, then our deeds were favourable in the eyes of the kings of the Hurrian troops. And between themselves they concluded a solid oath."

9 Von Dassow 2008, 54–56.
10 Torrecilla and Cohen 2018.
11 Skaist 1998; Cohen and Viano 2016. Cf. Yamada 2017.

The strong king heard about the tribute of our forefathers and the oath between them and he was respectful of the oath. He was willing to accept my greeting gift because of the words of the oath and because of our tribute.

Notes

a. The end of *ma-na-ḫa-*[*te*] followed by the sign ḪÉ has generated many explanations. See Dietrich and Loretz 1981, 216–217.

b. The form *in-na-ḫu-ú* has perplexed all who have dealt with the text. Some have suggested that the form is from *anāḫu*, others from *nâḫu*, both in the sense of 'to toil'. Others considered the verb *aḫû*, 'to be allied', which apart from this case in Idrimi's inscription, is not attested to in the N Stem. Whatever the case, it will suffice to consider a *figura etymologica* expression in our case, 'delivering what is to be delivered'; cf. Greenstein and Marcus 1976, 81. The verb *nâḫu* in the D stem can have the meaning of 'to bank', (CAD/N1: 149), in the sense of 'to put, place'. Compare Hebrew נוח, 'to rest', but in the Hiphil Stem, it can mean 'to cause to rest' (הֵנִיחַ) and 'to place, set down' (הִנִּיחַ). It is worth recalling Albright's suggestion (1957) regarding *mānaḫtu* in Ugarit, as 'gift', related to Hebrew *minha*(*t*) and Phoenician *mnht*, both derived from נוח, as well as Ugaritic *mnh*(*t*). So in the inscription, it is not too difficult to imagine, perhaps under West Semitic influence, the meaning we have suggested: the tribute (*mānaḫāte*) was delivered (*in-na-ḫu-ú*). This consideration allows us to explain another occurrence of the form *in-na-ḫu-ú*, appearing in line 41. See below.

c. Reading here *it-ti* seems to be the simplest solution, in a separative sense, 'to be respectful, fearful of, from', as the use of *itti* with *leqû*, 'to take from'. Cf. Dietrich and Loretz 1981, 218 and Durand 2011, 142, n. 155.

Let us now set the whole passage within the narration of the inscription. We learn that Parrattarna was hostile (*ú-na-kir-an-ni*) to Idrimi for seven years (ll. 43–44). Idrimi tells the reader how he solved this problem. He wrote to Parrattarna about the tribute (*ma-na-ḫa-te*) of his forefathers. He admitted that this tribute was given (*in-na-ḫu-ú*) by his forefathers regularly. This can be understood from the text, because it is implied that it happened over a period of time, under the successive kings of Mitanni. The supply of the tribute was enfolded with an oath, i.e., a treaty, between Idrimi's forefathers and the kings of Mitanni. After Parrattarna heard from Idrimi about the former agreements, he was willing to accept Idrimi's greeting gift (*šu-ul-mi-ia*). It probably was just the overture to the tribute, now renewed between the parties.

In short, we hear of how Idrimi ended the hostility with Mitanni by renewing the tribute his forefathers regularly paid, along with renewing the oath or treaty. Somewhat like what we read in the historical introduction to the Hittite treaties, Idrimi portrays himself as an equal to the Hurrian king. But of course, this was something that even he did not fully believe. If we go back a bit in the Inscription, to lines 36–42, we can read about Idrimi's relationship with other local kings. After Idrimi's "brothers" heard that all the Lands of Niya, Amae, Mukiš and Alalakh turned to him as one, they came before him and *it-ti-ia in-na-ḫu-ú* (l. 41), which we suggest to translate now, as 'they offered me (their tribute)'. For this reason, Idrimi offered them protection: *aḫ-ḫé*$^{\text{ḫi.a}}$ *aṣ-ṣur-šu-nu*, 'I protected the "brothers"'. A vassalage relationship had been created.

Hence, it is seen how Idrimi sets the stage for his submission to the Hurrian king. Wishing to diminish the negative impression that his capitulation to the demands of the Hurrians may have generated, he portrays himself as a king under which lay lower loyal vassals. Seeing what a great ruler he was, in return for his protection they were obliged to pay him tribute. And he, thus, in his turn, was not a third-rate vassal, but actually an almost-equal to the king of Mitanni.

After Idrimi promised to renew the tribute to Mitanni, he tells us that he increased the sacrifices (l. 55), and after retaking the oath, he became king of Alalakh (l. 58: lugal-*ku*). We suggest that these sacrifices may have been part of an official cult celebrated by or for the Mitanni state. Some circumstantial evidence of such a practice can be provided by the Urtenu letters. Recently, we have argued that the king of Ugarit was committed, along with Hittite officials, to assist in the performing a sort of an official state offerings, called the siskur.meš *malḫaššše*.[12] There are grounds to consider that this type of offering was not a Hittite innovation, but a practice common to Syria, possibly during the times of Mitanni rule.

In his discussion of the Idrimi Inscription, Na'aman (1980) summed up our passage thus. He suggested that the relationship between Idrimi and the Hurrian king was based on stipulations of a permanent nature, and that they were the kind of obligations Mitanni forced on its vassals. The clarification of the term *mānaḫātu* (as a plural form, differentiated from the singular of l. 103) in the inscription, as a type of tax or tribute reinforces Na'aman's conclusion. The enactment of sacrifices may also be considered as something of an official or state cult. Obviously, the evidence we have presented from Ugarit is not binding, and only circumstantial. One must take care not to infer from one to the other. But there is enough ground, both contextual and histori-

12 Cohen and Torricella 2020. See also Cohen 2011, for the state cult at Emar. Cf. Archi 2014.

cal, as argued, to accept our suggestions, and by so, gain one more step in the reconstruction of the history of imperial Mitanni about which so little is known.

References

Albright, William. F. 1957. "Recent Books on Assyriology and Related Subjects." *BASOR* 146: 34–35.

Archi, Alfonso. 2014. "Aštata: A Case of Hittite Imperial Religious Policy." *JANER* 14: 141–163.

Borger, R. 1968. "Die Statueinschrift des Idrimi von Alalach (um 1400 v. Chr.)." In *Textbuch zur Geschichte Israels*, edited by Kurt Galling, 21–24. Tübingen: Mohr Siebeck.

Cohen, Yoram. 2011. "The Administration of Cult in Hittite Emar." *AoF* 38: 145–157.

Cohen, Yoram and Eduardo Torrecilla. 2020. "Hittite Cult in Syria: Religious Imperialism or Religious Pluralism?" In *Cult, Temple, Sacred Spaces. Cult Practices and Cult Spaces in Hittite Anatolia and Neighbouring Cultures*. StBoT 66, edited by Suzanne Görke and Charles Steitler, 221–230. Wiesbaden: Harrassowitz.

Cohen, Yoram and Eduardo Torrecilla. Forthcoming. "The *mānaḫātu* and the End of Ugarit." BASOR.

Cohen, Yoram and Maurizio Viano. 2016. "A Land-grant Document from Emar: A Re-Edition and Discussion of LN-104 (aka GsKutscher 6)." KASKAL 13: 57–71.

del Olmo, Georgio and Joaquín Sanmartín. 2015. *A Dictionary of the Ugaritic Language in the Alphabetic Tradition*. Third, Revised Edition. HdO 112. Leiden—Boston: Brill.

Dietrich, Manfred and Oswald Loretz. 1981. "Die Inschrift des Königs Idrimi von Alalaḫ." *UF* 13: 201–278.

Durand, Jean-Marie. 2011. La fondation d'une lignée royale syrienne. Le geste d'Idrimi d'Alalah. In *Le jeune héros: Recherches sur la formation et la diffusion d'un thème littéraire au Proche-Orient ancient*. OBO 250, edited by Jean-Marie Durand, Thomas Römer, and Michaël Langlois, 94–150. Fribourg; Göttingen: Academic Press; Vandenhoeck & Ruprecht,.

George, Andrew R. 2003. *The Babylonian Gilgamesh Epic: Introduction, Critical Edition, and Cuneiform Texts*. Oxford—New York: Oxford University.

Greenstein, Edward L. and David Marcus. 1976. "The Akkadian Inscription of Idrimi." *JANES* 8, 59–96.

Lackenbacher, Silvie and Florence Malbran-Labat. 2016. *Lettres en Akkadien de la "Maison d'Urtēnu"*. RSO 23. Leuven: Peeters.

Lauinger, Jacob. 2021a. The Electronic Idrimi. http://oracc.museum.upenn.edu/aemw/alalakh/idrimi/. Accessed 18th March 18, 2022.

Lauinger, Jacob. 2021b. "Discourse and Meta-discourse in the Statue of Idrimi and Its Inscription." *MAARAV* 23: 19–38.

Longman, Tremper III. 1997. "The Autobiography of Idrimi (1.148)." In *The Context of Scripture: Canonical Compositions from the Biblical World*, Volume 1, edited by William Hallo and K. Lawson Younger, 479–480. Leiden: Brill.

Na'aman, N. 1980. "A Royal Scribe and His Scribal Products in the Alalakh IV Court." *OA* 19: 107–116.

Oller, Gary. H. 1977. "The Autobiography of Idrimi: A New Text Edition with Philological and Historical Commentary." PhD diss., University of Pennsylvania.

Oppenheim, A. Leo. 1969. "The Story of Idrimi, King of Alalakh." In *The Ancient Near East in Texts Relating to the Old Testament*, edited by James Pritchard, 557–558. Princeton, NJ: Princeton University Press.

Skaist, Aharon. 1998. "A Hurrian Term in Emar." In *General Studies and Excavations at Nuzi 10/2*. SCCNH 9, edited by David I. Owen and Gernot Wilhelm, 169–171. Bethesda, MD: CDL.

Smith, Sidney. 1949. *The Statue of Idri-mi*. Occasional Publications of the British Institute of Archaeology in Ankara, no. 1. London: British Institute of Archaeology in Ankara.

Torrecilla, Eduardo and Yoram Cohen. 2018. "A Mittani Letter Order from Azu (HAD 8) and Its Implications for the Chronology and History of the Middle Euphrates Region in the Late Bronze Age." RA 112: 149–158.

Vita, Juan Pablo. 2021. "The Hittites in the Administrative Texts of Ugarit." KASKAL 18, 111–126.

Von Dassow, Eva. 2008. *State and Society in the Late Bronze Age Alalah under the Mittani Empire*. SCCNH 17. Bethesda, MD: CDL.

Yamada, Mashamichi. 2017. "The Arana Documents from Emar Revisited." *Orient* 52, 121–133.

CHAPTER 4

On Aramaic Loanwords in Neo- and Late-Babylonian Texts: Morphophonological Classification, Documentary Distribution, General Evaluation, and Conclusions (Part Two)

Ran Zadok | ORCID: 0000-0002-9758-4545
Tel Aviv University
zadokr@tauex.tau.ac.il

Abstract

This study is the second part of Zadok (2021a). This part presents a morphophonological classification of the data of Aramaic loanwords in Neo- and Late-Babylonian. It offers a general evaluation which consists of a socio-historical background of the periods in question, chronology, provenance, and distribution according to various criteria. A conclusion closes the study.

Keywords

Aramaic – Akkadian – Neo-Babylonian – Late Babylonian – Loanwords – Late Babylonian society and history

תקציר

המאמר הנוכחי הוא חלק ב׳ של Zadok (2021a). בחלק זה אנו נציג ניתוח מורפולוגי של מילים ארמיות השאולות לנאו-בבלית ולבבלית מאוחרת. הדיון כולל רקע היסטורי חברתי, כרונולוגיה, מקום ממצא, ותפוצה על פי קריטריונים שונים. הדיון מסתיים בסיכום.

מילות מפתח

ארמית – אכדית – נאו-בבלית – בבלית מאוחרת – מילים שאולות – היסטוריה וחברה בתקופה הבבלית המאוחרת

 | DOI:10.1163/9789004526822_005

المستخلص

هذه الدّراسة هي عبارة عن جزء ثان ل(Zadok (2021a. في هذا الجزء يتمّ عرض التّحليل الصّرفيّ لكلمات آراميّة استعيرت في اللّغة البابليّة الحديثة واللّغة البابليّة المتأخّرة. يشمل البحث خلفيّة تاريخيّة واجتماعيّة، التّسلسل الزمنيّ، مصدر المعطيات وتوزيعها حسب معايير مختلفة. ينتهي البحث بخلاصة.

الكلمات المفتاحيّة

الآراميّة – الأكديّة – اللّغة البابليّة الحديثة – اللّغة البابليّة المتأخّرة – الكلمات المستعارة – تاريخ الدّولة البابليّة المتأخّرة ومجتمعها

This study is the second part of Zadok (2021a), which appeared in the *Israel Oriental Studies Annual*, volume 21. The first part of this study provided an introduction to the topic and then offered a detailed semantic-topical taxonomy of the Aramaic loan words. This part presents a morphophonological classification of the data of Aramaic loadwords in Neo- and Late-Babylonian texts. It then offers an evaluation which includes a sociohistorical overview, a chronological and a geographical distribution of the loanwords, the loadwords according to their parts of speech, and their distribution according to semantic-topical grouping. A conclusion closes the study.[1]

II Morphophonological Classification

II.a *Substantives and Adjectives*

II.a.1 Nominal Formations

II.a.1.1. Q*V*tl

II.a.1.1.1 *Qatl*

II.a.1.1.1.1 *With Stable Consonants*

bad-qu (↑I.d.7), *qa-áš-bi* (↑I.b.3), *s/šap-qu* (↓II.c.1.1.1).

1 For the abbreviations, see Zadok 2021a, 72. References to the Introduction are marked below as "0". The indices to this study are found here: https://drive.google.com/file/d/1FgsBKlhi_VtkLZWMyxrUk9OjgiihpToC/view?usp=sharing

II.a.1.1.1.2 *With Resonant Consonants*

dar-gu (↑I.d.7), *ga-lu-tu* (← *galy*, verbal adj.) "captives" (collective "captivity", ↑I.k), ^{lú}*hal-pi/pu, hal-pu-'* (↑I.h), *ka-an-šú* (↑I.e), *na-áš-ru* (↑I.c.1), ^{na4}*qá-ad-ru* (↑I.d.5), *šal-ṭu* (↑I.d.2), *ia-ar-qa-nu*^{sar} (↑I.b.2), *ka-as-lu* (→ *ka-sal/sa-al*, pl. *ka-sa-al-la-an-nu*, ↑I.j).

II.a.1.1.1.3 *With a Guttural Consonant and a Resonant*

a-ra (↑0), *p[a]-'-lu* "work" (*si vera lectio*, to P-ʿ-L),[2] *a-lu-ú* (↑I.d.7).

II.a.1.1.1.4 Qaty

ga-du-ú (↑I.c.1),[3] *ha-nu-ut-tu*$_4$ (↑I.d.7).

II.a.1.1.1.5 Qa'l

**ra'š—ra-šá-nu, ra-šá-(a)-ni* (with Akkad. pl., ↑I.h), i.e., with *a'* → *ā*.[4]

II.a.1.1.2 *Qitl* (→ *Qetl*)

II.a.1.1.2.1 *With Stable Consonants*

zi-ip-tu$_4$ (↑I.d.1).

II.a.1.1.2.2 *With Resonant Consonants* (*Partially* → qitVl *Due to Resonant* l/r)

^{na4}*gi-iz-re-e-ti* (↑I.d.4); *pi-ir-qú-ti(-šú-nu,*↑I.f); *gi-id-mu*, and with anaptyxis *gi-di-mu/im* (↑I.b.3); *ki-ir-ka/ki-iš-ki* (↑I.d.3, with the NB/LB shift *rk* → *šk*); *si-ip-ru/si-pi-ri* (↑I.a); *si-ir-pi/pu, sír-pu, sér-pu*^{me} (*si-ra-pi/pu*, ↑I.d.4),[5] *gi-il-du/gi-la-du* (↑I.d.2), *migdu* (↑I.b.4) and *ṣe-er-pu* (↑I.d.3).

II.a.1.1.2.3 *With a (Proto-)guttural Consonant and a Resonant*

he-šá-ru-ú: *ešrû* with anaptyxis, which is not uncommon in *qVtl*-formations (↑I.e).

2 A letter which was sent from Babylon by Bēl-iddina to Sargon, reporting about work in temples throughout Babylonia including the Sealand; Dietrich 2003, 41, 43; Streck 2018, 60.

3 JBA and Mand. *g'dyh* are based on this formation, but a rare form, *gydyh*, "his kid" is also recorded in Sassanian Babylonia, i.e., with *a* → *i*, like in later Levantine Arab. *jidi*; Müller-Kessler 2011, 227 *ad* 260. A forerunner of the latter may be extant in the second component of the toponym Βηθαγιδεα referring to a place in the northern Negev, a region with a predominantly early Arab population, as early as the Byzantine period, if not before; Avi-Yonah 1976, 36.

4 For the early shift *r'š'* → *ryš'*, see Bar-Asher Siegal 2016, 79:3.1.3.1; cf. NA ^{lú}*re-'-sa-ni*.

5 Payne 2013, YBC 3941, 17 (two *s.*) from the Eanna archive; Uruk, 38 Nbk. II = 567/6 BC. See Zadok 2021c, 125–126.

II.a.1.1.2.4 *With a (Proto-)guttural Consonant*

pi-hi-iz (with anaptyxis, ↑I.l); *ek/ik-bi* (↑I.f).

II.a.1.1.2.5 Qitw (qetw)/qutw

ṭi/ṭu-ru-ú (↑I.b.1); *še-ru-ú* (↑I.c.2).

II.a.1.1.3 *Qutl*

II.a.1.1.3.1 *With Stable Consonants*

pu-uš-ku (↑I.e).

II.a.1.1.3.2 *With Resonant Consonants*

gub/gu-ub-na-tu$_4$ (↑I.c.2); *ṣu-ur-bi*^{sar} (↑I.b.2); *bu-qul* (↑I.b.4, with anaptyxis); *ur-ba-(an-)ni* (↑I.d.6); *uš-ru-ú* (↑I.e).

II.a.1.1.3.3 *With a Guttural Consonant and a Resonant*

^{uzu}*un-qu* (↑I.c.2) and with anaptyxis *hu-ši-ni* (↑I.l).

II.a.1.1.3.4 Qu'l

bu-'-šu (↑I.b.4).

II.a.1.1.3.5 Quty

^{túg}*gu-la-nu*, ^{túg}*gu-le-en/nu*, *gu-le-e-ni*, pl. ^{túg}*gu-le-né-e* (↑I.d.3). Both the base and the suffix (originally *-ān*) are substantival. Except for *gu-la-nu*, is the *-e-* (/*ē*/) due to *imāla*? This phenomenon is found in the originally *qātil*-active participles as *sēpiru*, "alphabet scribe", *nēkisu* for *nākisu* and *ṭē'inu* ← *ṭā'inu*, "miller". The nominal pattern *qutl-ān* produces substantives (with *-ān* → *-ēn*).[6]

II.a.1.2 Q*V*t*V*l

II.a.1.2.1 *Qatal*

II.a.1.2.1.1 *With Stable Consonants*

za-ka-ka-tu$_4$, *za-ku-ku-tú* (↑I.d.1). The latter is a variant with ⟨*u*⟩ (/*o*/?).

II.a.1.2.1.2 *With Resonant Consonants*

^{šim}*ba-al-tam-mu*/⌜*ba-al-ta*⌝*-am* (↑I.b.1); *šá-ma-ka-a-ta* (pl., ↑I.b.4), in OSyr. *qatl* (→ pl. *qatal*?; the variation may be due to the resonant); *ba-ga-ni-'*, "invocation, cry, call" (cf. Late Aram. *bgn*, OSyr. B-G-N, "to call");[7] *ga-la-la* (↑I.a).

6 Brockelmann 1908 [1961], 391:213; 412–413:225, B, 2dβγγ.

7 Hackl et al. 2014, 176:61, 25 and 268–269:152, rev. 5′. See Degen 1974, 99, 103–104. Since the *n* is

II.a.1.2.2 *Qatil*

a-ṭi-ri (↑I.d.7), *ia-hi-il-ti* (↑I.c.1), *ha-di-ri* and eventually $^{\text{lú}\ulcorner}$*ha-ad/ṭ-ri, ha-ad/ṭ-ru, ha-d/ṭa-ri, ha-dar/ṭár* (*qatl*-formation with anaptyxis, ↑I.h).

II.a.1.2.3 *Qitil*

ki-ni-iš-tu_4, *ki-niš-*tu_4*/ti, ki-na-áš-*tu_4*/ti*, ^{lú}*ki-na-al-tú/*tu_4*/ti*, and ^{lú}*ki-nar-ti* (the last form originates from *kinalti*, with dissimilation of *liquida*, ↑I.h). The early attestation from Sūhu (mid 8th century BC), viz., ^{lú}*ki-na-al-ta*, is rendered as "workforce".[8]

II.a.1.3 Qātil (→ qātel, qetīl)

II.a.1.3.1 With Stable Consonants

^{f}*sa-gi-it-*tu_4, *sa-git-tú* (with fem. *-t* and assimilation of the preceding *d*, ↑I.i); ^{lú}*qa-ṭe-e* (pl., ↑I.d.6).

II.a.1.3.2 With Resonant Consonants

ia-a-ri-tu, ia-a-ri-tu-tu (the latter with the abstact suff. *-ūt*, ↑I.f).

II.a.1.3.3 With a (Proto-)guttural Consonant and a Resonant

ha-li-il/li/lu, hal-li-li (with ⟨*a*CC⟩ for /*ā*C/), and with Akkadian pl. *ha-li/lil-la-nu* (cf. [*h*]*a-li-li*^{meš}/*hal-li-li*^{meš}, ↑I.d.4).[9]

II.a.1.3.4 With a (Proto-)guttural Consonant

^{lú}*pa-te-eh* (↑I.i).

II.a.1.3.5 With *Imāla*

se-pi-ru (I.a), cf. *bēhiru* (↑o). Bēl-ēṭir (^{d}+EN-SUR) son of Nabû-šarra-uṣur, the alphabet scribe (*sepīru*) of the *sukkallu*-official (^{lú}*su-kal-la*), has a paternal name with *šarru*. His title is spelled ^{lú}*sep-pi-ri*, i.e., with ⟨(C)*ep-pi-*⟩ for /*ēp*/.[10]

II.a.1.4 Qawtal

Produces substantives,[11] viz. *uṣ-ṣa-ra, ú-ṣa-ri* (↑I.d.7).

---

not geminated, a segmentation *b+ gn* (to G-N-N "protect") is unlikely; Schaeder 1938, cf. Abraham and Sokoloff 2011, 27:21. An Old Iranian etymology, suggested by Eilers 1936 and followed by Goshen-Gottstein 1970, 7, is to be rejected.

8 Frame 1995, 298:1002, 2, iii, 13; Hess 2021, 1424, n. 109.

9 Zadok 2020, 4.

10 He acted as the second witness; Borsippa, Rēʾi-alpe archive, 6.v.24 Dar. I = 498 BC, HSM 1895.1.12, 15 ff.

11 Brockelmann 1908 [1961], 344:130.

II.a.1.5 *QVtV:l*

Vowel lengthening is expressed orthographically in NB/LB either by V-V or VC-C, but this cannot be generalized, for quite often both means just render a stress.[12]

II.a.1.5.1 *qatāl*

ba-al-tam-mu (↑I.b.1), *ha-ra-ra* (↑I.f).

II.a.1.5.2 *Qatīl*

II.a.1.5.2.1 *With Stable Consonants*

ga-bi-bi (↑I.j)

II.a.1.5.2.2 *With Resonant Consonants*

da-ri-ka/ki/ku (↑I.b.3); *ga-ri-ṣa-tu*$_4$ (↑I.b.5); *gam-mi-da-tu*$_4$, ^{túg}*gam-mi-da-ti*, *gam-mi-da-a-ti* (↑I.d.3); *na-si-ki/ku*, *na-sik* (pl. *na-si-ka-a-ti*, *na-si-ka-tu*), ^{f}*na-si-ka-tu*$_4$ (↑I.h); *sa-pi-na-tú/tu*$_4$, *sa-pi-in-na-a-ta* (with 〈*i*CC〉 = /*ī*C/, *sa-pa-na-a-tú* is probably a scribal error for *sa-pi-na-a-tú*, ↑I.k); *ta-mi-im/mi*, *ta-am-mi-im*, fem. *ta-mì-mi-tu*$_4$, pl. *ta-mi-me-e*, *ta-mi-im-ma-a-ta* (↑I.c.1).

II.a.1.5.2.3 *With a (Proto-)guttural Consonant and a Resonant*

^{šim}*šá-li-ha-tu*$_4$, ^{šim}*šal-ha-at* (↑I.b.1).

II.a.1.5.2.4 *With a (Proto-)guttural Consonant*

ha-ṭi-ṭi, pl. *ha-ṭi-ṭa-ni* (↑I.d.7); *ma-ṣi-hi* (↑I.j);[13] ^{šim}*ka-ṣi-ʾ-a-tu*$_4$, ^{šim}*ka-ṣi-a-tú/tu*$_4$, ^{šim}*ka-ṣa-a-a-tú* (↑I.b.1, + fem. *-at*).

II.a.1.5.2.5 Qatīl → Qetīl (*with Attenuation of a Short Unstressed* a)

ga/ge-ri-ṣa-te (along with *ga-ri-ṣa-tu*$_4$, I.b.5); *ge-ṭi-pi* (↑I.b.6); *he-si-il-ti* (↑I.c.1); *ke/qé-ši-ir-tu*$_4$ (↑I.b.1). Regarding *qé-ši-šú* (↑I.h), the Aramaic form is of the *qattīl*-formation, which is basically interchangeable with *qatīl*.[14]

II.a.1.5.3 *Qatūl*

II.a.1.5.3.1 *With a (Proto-)guttural Consonant*

^{lú}*ia-a-hu-da-nu* (Akkad. pl., ↑I.g).

---

12 Zadok 1978, 250:4123.

13 Beyer 1984, 629, s.v. *mṣyʿ*, regarded it as a alternatively a *qattīl*-formation, but he later (1994, 377,; id. 2004, 435) took it as a *qatīl*-formation.

14 Sokoloff 2017, 582 and Zadok 2021c, 125:2.

II.a.1.5.3.2 *With a Resonant*
ra-qu-un-du (↑I.d.4, alternatively to *qattūl*).

II.a.1.5.4 *Qitīl*
*ši-bit-tu*₄, *ši-bít-tu*₄^sar (↑I.b.2).

II.a.1.5.5 *Qutāl*
ṣu-ra-ru, ú-za-ru/ri (↑I.d.3) and perhaps *qu-na-a-ta* (↑I.b.4).

II.a.1.5.6 *Qutūl*
^lú*gu-du-du* (↑0) and perhaps *ṣu-ru-ú* (↑I.b.3); *nu-qu-pu-tu* (alternatively to *qut-tūl*, ↓II.a.1.6.6.1).

II.a.1.6 Q*V*tt*V*(:)l
II.a.1.6.1 *Qattāl*
II.a.1.6.1.1 *With a Resonant Consonant*
^lú*ha-A+A-la*^me, JPA *ḥyyl* (↑I.g), *hal-*⌈*lap*⌉ (↑I.h).

II.a.1.6.1.2 *With a (Proto-)guttural Consonant*
aq-qa-bu-ú (↑I.b.5), ^lú*ha-am-qa-du-ú-a* (↑I.i).

II.a.1.6.1.3 *With Dissimilation of Emphatics*
qàṭ-ṭa-A+A (↑I.d.6). [with GAD = gaṭ]

II.a.1.6.2 *Qattīl*
II.a.1.6.2.1 *With a (Proto-)guttural Consonant*
^uzu*hat-ti-ik* (↑I.c.2).

II.a.1.6.2.2 *With a (Proto-)guttural Consonant and a Resonant*
sa-ar-ri-ih (↑I.d.3).

II.a.1.6.3 *Qattūl*
la-mu-ta-nu, la-ú-ta-[*ni-šú*], *lam-mu-ta-nu* (↑I.h).

II.a.1.6.4 *Quttal*
^ú*šul-lam-mat* (↑I.b.1).

II.a.1.6.5 *Quttul*
ṭùl-lu-um-ma-'-u (↑I.f).

II.a.1.6.6 *Quttūl*

II.a.1.6.6.1 *With Resonant Consonants*

nu-qu-pu-tu (↑I.b.6, + *-ūt*, alternatively to *qutūl*, ↑II.a.1.5.6).

II.a.1.6.6.2 *With a (Proto-)guttural Consonant*

su-'-ú-du (↑I.l).

II.a.1.7 QVl

II.a.1.7.1 *Qal*

II.a.1.7.1.1 *With a (Proto-)guttural Consonant*

adû (↑I.f).

II.a.1.7.1.2 *With an Initial Semi-vowel*

lú*ia-a-da-'*, lú*ia-a-du-'*(meš), (lú)*'-ú-du* (presumably with *a* → *o*), *'-du* (I.e).

II.a.1.8 QV:l

II.a.1.8.1 *Qāl*

ma-hat (**mʿt*, ↑I.e)

II.a.1.8.2 *Qīl*

lú*gi-ra*-A+A (with *-āy*, ↑I.a).

II.a.1.8.3 *Qūl*

gu-da-nu (Akkad. pl. of **gūdu*, ↑I.d.2); *ṣu-pa-a-ta* (pl., ↑I.d.3); *pu-ú-lu* (↑I.b.4); and *zu-ú-pu*sar (with aphaeresis, ↑I.b.2).

II.a.1.9 Qaw/yl

II.a.1.9.1 *Qawl*

kuš*nu-ú-ṭu* (Akkad. pl. kuš*nu-ṭa-nu*) in view of CA *nawṭ* (↑I.d.2).

II.a.1.9.2 *Qayl*

II.a.1.9.2.1 *With Stable C_1 and C_3*

za-'-tu₄, *za-A+A-it*, *za-(a)-'-it* (↑I.b.1); the last two spellings are with a syllabic extension, which is a late phenomenon.[15]

15 Zadok 1978, 433–434, 255–257; cf. Bravmann 1977, 100–103 and Qimron 1983, 17.

II.a.1.9.2.2 *With a Resonant Last Radical*

^{lú}*hi-ia-(a-)lu*, ^{lú}*hi-a-lu*, *hi-ʾ-a-lu*, pl. ^{lú}*hi-ia(-a)-la-a-nu*, ^{lú}*hi-ʾ(-a)-la-a-nu*, ^{lú}*hi-ia-a-la-ni*, *ḥyyln* (↑I.g). It is originally a *qayl*-formation; Abraham and Sokoloff (2011, 35b:92); later *qyal* → *qyāl*.[16]

II.a.1.10 Q*V*ll

II.a.1.10.1 *Qall*

II.a.1.10.1.1 *With Stable Consonants*

ga-ab-bu (↑I.c.2), *kap-pi* (↑I.e).

II.a.1.10.1.2 *With a Resonant Consonant*

ga-an(-ni), *ga-an-na-ta/ti* (↑I.c.2, I.j);[17] *ta-am-ma-tu₄* (fem.; the mas. is of the *qatīl*-formation, ↑I.c.1); ^{kuš}*ṣa-al-la*, ^{kuš}*ṣal-la/lu*, *ṣal-lu* (Akkad. pl. ^{kuš}*ṣal-la-nu*, *ṣal-la-a-nu*; cf. ^{kuš}*ṣal-lu*^{meš}, ↑I.d.2).

With dissimilatory *n*: ^{dug}*kan-da*, ^{dug}*kan-du*, *kan-du*$_x$, ^{dug}*kan-da-a-nu* (with Akkad. pl.) and *ki-in-du* (with *qall* → *qill*, ↑I.d.5).

II.a.1.10.1.3 *With a (Proto-)guttural Consonant and a Resonant*

hal-la (↑I.b.5); *hal-la-tú*, *hal-la-a-ta*, ^{giš}MÁ *hal-la-*⌜*a-tu*⌝ (↑I.d.6), *hal-la-a-ta*, *hal-la-tu₄*, *hal-lat* (↑I.j).

II.a.1.10.2 *Qill*

ki-in-du (↑I.d.5; cf. ↑II.a.1.10.1.2).

II.a.1.10.3 *Qull*

II.a.1.10.3.1 *With Stable Consonants*

gu-ub-ba-a-ni (with Akkad. pl., ↑I.j), *gu-ub-ba-tu₄* (↑I.d.6).

II.a.1.10.3.2 *With Resonant Consonants*

gu-mat/gu-ma-ti (↑I.j).

II.a.1.11 Q*V*lq*V*l

II.a.1.11.1 *Qalqal*

har-har-ra (↑I.f).

---

16 Muraoka 1976.

17 For *-at* as a hypothetical diminutive marker in limited cases, see von Soden, GAG, 91:60a and Streck 2010, 288:1.1, 290:2.2.

II.a.1.11.2 *Qalqīl*
za-an-zi-ri (↑I.c.1).

II.a.1.12 ʾ-: Aqtāl → Q(ə)tāl
he-sa-(a-)nu, he-sa-an-nu/ni, and *ah/eh-he-sa-nu* (↑I.f).

II.a.1.13 m-
II.a.1.13.1 *Maqtal*
ma-as-tar (↑I.d.7), *man-de-et/ti* ← **maddaʿ-t* (↑I.k), to W/Y-D-ʿ with dissimilatory *-n-* and *-a-* → *-e-* due to -/ ʿ/; *man-ṭa-ri* (↑I.b.3). Early NB *man-de-si* is recorded in a letter whose sender was presumably an Assyrian.[18]

II.a.1.13.2 *Maqal*
kuš*ma-gal-lat,* kuš*ma-gal-la-tú, ma-gal-la-a* (↑I.a).

II.a.1.13.3 *Muqattil*
Mumarriqānu, "guarantor who guarantees that property sold is alienable" (↑I.f, D active participle + *-ān*).[19] E.g., *mu-mar-ri-qa-an,* or *mu-mar-raq-an(-na)/mu-mar-raq-qa-an-nu* with the CVC-sign RAQ, which is indifferent to vowel quality; **muwarriqān* → *allegro*-forms: *mu-ur-qa-an-nu,* with *-ān* → *-ōn, mu-ru-qu-na/nu,* and with omission of *-ān*: *mu-ur-raq, mu-ru-qu, mu-ur-qu,* all from Seleucid Uruk.

II.a.1.14 Yanqūl → Yaqqūl
ú*ia-bu-ṭu* (↑I.b.4).

II.b *Pronouns*

Only *a-ga-a* (proximal demonstrative "this, that" ← Aram. *hk* with V*k*V→ V*g*V);[20] and *ki-ma-ʾ* (interrogative "how much/many"? ← Aram. *kmʾ/h*).[21]

II.c *Verbs*

Most verbs belong to the G stirps (unmarked). Only five are of the D one (Ḥ-D-Ṯ, M-R-Q, Q-B-L, S-B-S, and ʿ-D-Y). One (G-L-Y) is of the Š stirps, but another verb (S-G-Y) which is frequently recorded in G, is also attested in Š.

18 Hess 2021, 1425 + n. 112.
19 For the pattern participle + *-ān,* see Streck 2005, 233–239.
20 Fales 1980, 264; cf. LB *še-ra-ag-gu-ʾ*; see Zadok 2021b. Aram. *hk* /*hāk*/ is not extant in *akanna,* "here", which is already recorded in MB; CAD A/1: 260–261; Abraham and Sokoloff 2011, 25; Hess 2021, 1412, n. 63.
21 Von Soden 1966, 13; id. 1977, 189; AHw.: 477b, 1568; Abraham and Sokoloff 2011, 37:108.

The N stirps is represented only by N-Ṭ-L. None of the forms which are defined as Gt is listed as such in Streck (2003). It is noteworthy that the thematic vowels of the *iprVs*-conjugation of the G stirps are at least in three cases not identical with those in the Aramaic documentation; such are *irdip* vs. JBA and OSyr. *yrdwp*, and **ipraq* (extant in *l-ipraq*) vs. OSyr. *yprwq*.[22] Regarding *i-se-du-'*, it may be based on **yasʿad*, with the colouring of the thematic vowel due to the guttural, although Aram. (JPA) has *ysʿwd*.

The basically *yaqtul*-conjugation (with *-w-*) was presumably motivated by the fact that all the three verbs are fientic-dynamic and transitive. The pertinent forms of *mâru* (M-W/Y-R), viz. *a-mir-ri, a-mir-ram-ma, a-mi-ri-am-ma* are compatible with an Akkadian G stirps, but their thematic vowel betrays an originally Aramaic C stirps; cf. JBA *ʾmyr*, lit. "exchange" (vs. *ʾmwr* with an approximate denotation). However, SA has forms with *i* also in the G stirps, namely *nmyr, tmyrwn*; Tal (2000, 457). Note that *nmyr* has a variant *nmwr*, which raises the suspicion that it is an orthographic error. G of Ḫ-Ṭ-Ṭ (*iḫ-ṭu-uṭ* vs. OSyr. *yḥwṭ*) is adjusted to the conjugation of verbs with identical 2nd and 3rd radicals.

II.C.1 G Stirps

II.C.1.1 *Strong Verbs*

II.C.1.1.1 With Stable Consonants

sapāqu (SB from NB Uruk *ta-sa-pi-iq*) is thought to originate from Aram. Ś-P-Q, "to be sufficient, to abound" or "to be able, to have power" (OSyr. *spq*).[23] NB and SB generally render West Sem. /ś/ by ⟨*š*⟩, but from the 6th century BC onwards Aram. /ś/ started shifting to /s/.

II.C.1.1.2 With One Resonant Consonant

katāru: *ak-te-ra-ma*; *sa-lu-ú* (↑I.l); *parāqu* (P-R-Q); *lip-ra-aq* ("let PN isolate" referring to the Arameans, early NB Nippur);[24] *radāpu*: *ir-dip-ma*; Gt *ar-te-di-ip(-šú-nu-tu), niš-te-di-ip(-šú-nu-tu)*,[25] *rad-pu* (↑I.g);[26] *salāqu*: *i-se-li-iq-qu* (↑I.j); *sepēru*: *si-ip-ri* [kur]*Ár-ma-*[A+A *lu*]*-us-pi-ir-ma* (↑I.a).

---

22 Both *a-o* and *a-a* are transitive-fientic; Aro 1964, 141.

23 Abraham and Sokoloff 2011, 49:207; for the NA occurrences, see Cherry 2017, 241–243. It renders Akkad. *danānu* "to become strong". A derived substantive is SB *s/šap-qu* (also from NB Uruk, in a medical commentary) which is equated with Akkad. *dannu* "strong"; CAD S: 167; cf. OSyr. *spq'*, "able, powerful".

24 Cole, *Nippur*, 27, 18; CAD P: 161; Streck 2007, 150.

25 With *rt* → *št*, common in NB/LB.

26 Sokoloff 1974, 154 *ad* 32, 8; Hackl 2021a, 1449.

II.C.1.1.3 With Two Resonant Consonants

parāmu, "to rend, slice through" (NB, lit., ↑I.b.5): *pa-ar-mu*, "(whose shoe-soles) are in tatters", *pa-ri-im*, SB *ta-par-ra-am* (medical) ← Aram. P-R-M, "to cut apart, tear to pieces".[27] R-K-L: *ni-ir-ki-il-ma* (↑I.e).

II.C.1.1.4 With a Resonant and a (Proto-)guttural Consonant

ha-ár-ku (ʿ-R-K, ↑ I.g); *behēru*: NB (Sargonid) *ib-te-hir* (*bihirtu* ~), *ta-bi-ih-hir* (↑I.g); *karāʾu* (K-R-ʿ): *ak-ta-ra-ʾ* (Gt, ↑ I.l).

II.C.1.1.5 With Two Resonants and a (Proto-)guttural Consonant

lehēmu: *al-he-me, il-hi-im* (↑I.l) ← Aram. L-Ḥ-M contaminated by Akkadian *lêmu.*

II.C.1.1.6 With a (Proto-)guttural Consonant

sêdu (S-ʿ-D): *i-se-du-ʾ, is-se-dan-ni/nu* (↑I.l ← Aram. *sʿdny*).

II.C.1.2 Verba Primae n

N-T-N is extant in the hybrid form *na-tan-ta-áš-šú*,[28] i.e., Aram. G pf. 2nd sg. m. *natantā* +Akkad. dative pronoun "you gave to him," actually in an idiomatic expression *hulluqu n.* "you have allowed him to escape".[29]

II.C.1.3 Verba Mediae Infirmae

mâru (M-W/Y-R): *a-mir-ri, a-mir-ram-ma, a-mi-ri-am-mai*, "exchange" (↑I.e).

II.C.1.4 Verba Ultimae Infirmae

II.C.1.4.1 With a Resonant Consonant

šelû (Š-L-W/Y): *a-šel-lu, niš-lu-ú, ta-šel-la/li/lu, ta-šel-la-ʾ/a*$_4$ (↑I.l); *še-ru-ú*: *iš-te-ri* (G perf. 3rd sg. m. of Š-R-Y, i.e., "he has redeemed");[30] *ṭerû* B (Ṭ -R-Y): *ṭa-re-e šá* PN$_1$ PN$_2$ *iṭ-ru-ú*, "the beating that PN$_1$ struck PN$_2$"; *ṭarrû*, "beating, assault" (↑I.l); *ra-qu*^{1} (?), *i-re-ʾ* from R-Ḍ-W/Y → R-Q-Y → R- ʿ-Y, "to wish" (↑I.l).'

II.C.1.4.2 With a Resonant and a (Proto-)guttural Consonant

IA-*ʾ-lu* (to ʿ-L-Y, ↑ I.e) "charged against, drafted to the debit". The polyphonic sign IA renders not only /*ya*/, but also /*ye*/ or /*yi*/; thus, it neither confirms

27 CAD P: 161; Cherry 2017, 204–205.

28 Cole, *Nippur*, 81, 27.

29 Hess 2021, 1422.

30 Abraham and Sokoloff 2011, 24–25, n. 31:21.

nor infirms any attempt to establish the quality of the Aramaic preformative vowel.[31]

II.C.1.4.3 With a (Proto-)guttural Consonant

qaṭû "to approach" (Q-Ṭ-'): *i-quṭ-ṭu-ú* (↑I.g; the CVC sign QUṬ is indifferent to vowel quality), cf. OSyr. *qṭ'*, "to wander about"; *segû* (S-G-Y), "to move about": *i-seg-ga, i-seg-gu-ú; ul i-se-eg-gu-ú, ni-se-eg-gu-ú*, Gt *is-se-eg-gu, is-se-gi*; → "to observe laws" (← "pursue", in the Achaemenid royal inscriptions, ↑ I.k), *a-se-eg-gu, i-se-gu-ú, si-i-gi* (imperative); causative ("to let someone go"): *ú-šá-as-gu-ú*(-šú); "to enforce a law" (Achaemenid inscription of Darius I): *se-gu-ú* "roaming, moving" (adj., *sēgû*, SB).

II.C.1.5 *Verbs with Identical 2nd and 3rd Radicals*

ha-pa-ap, "rubbing/washing" (of stone, G inf.);[32] *haṭāṭu* "to dig" (Ḫ-Ṭ-Ṭ): SB *ah/ih-ṭu-uṭ*; NB ~, *ah/ih-ṭu-uṭ-ma, ih-ṭu-ṭu-ma, hu-uṭ-ṭa-a-ma* (↑I.d.7).

II.C.1.6 *Defective Verbs*

a-pu-ú (*'-P-Y*) is followed by *ṭe-hu-ú* "to smear" (Borsippa; also LB Uruk [lú]*ṭe-hu-ú*, pl. [lú]*ṭe-hi-ia* "smearers"; ↑ I.b.5);[33] *ibinna, binna* (W/Y-H-B), *ibi-inna* (etc.) "give!", earliest occurrence, Dēr, 11 Sar. II = 711 BC, a compendious kudurru.[34]

II.C.2 D Stirps

II.C.2.1 *Strong Verbs*

II.C.2.1.1 With Stable Consonants

subbusu, "to collect, assemble" (S-B-S): *ú-sa-ab-bi-is; su-ub-bu-su-tu*, D verbal adj. pl. m. "gathered, assembled" (↑I.h).

II.C.2.1.2 With Resonant Consonants

qu-ub-bu-ul/lu, qu-ub-bal, fem. *qu-ub-ul-la-at* (D stative of Q-B-L, "received", ↑I.e); *murruqu*, "to clear (a sold property) from claims" (M-R-Q, ↑I.f): *mu-ur-ru-qu* (← *mu-ur-qu/mu-ru-uq*), *ú-mar-raq-, ú-mar-raq-qu-ú, tu-mar-raq-am, un-dar-ri-qu* (with *-mt-* → *-nd-* which is common in NB/LB); *mumarriqānu*

---

31 Gzella 2014, 95–96 and Sandowicz 2019, 4.

32 Ebabbar archive, 1.II.9 Nabonidus = 547 BC; VS 6, 77, 8.

33 CAD Ṭ: 83, supplementing Abraham and Sokoloff 2011, 55: 261. For background, see Waerzeggers 2010, 116 + n. 520, 198, 213, 228–230, 332, 334; Zadok 2009, 197.

34 VS 1, 70 = Paulus 2014, 719: ŠU II 1, iv, 21. For 717, ii, 13, consider an alternative reading, *Šá-ma-ia* which is more common in NB/LB (and see Hackl 2012) and may be an old hypocoristic (with an abbreviated base) of an Akkadian compound anthroponym with *Šamaš*; 718, iii, 10 has the surname I–*sin*–A+A.

"guarantor who guarantees that property sold is alienable"; the form is a D active participle plus a substantivizing *-ān*, e.g., *mu-mar-ri-qa-an*, or *mu-mar-raq-an(-na)/mu-mar-raq-qa-an-nu*. It originates from **muwarriqān* and has the allegro-forms *mu-ur-qa-an-nu*, *mu-ru-qu-na/nu* (with *-ān* → *-ōn*) and *mu-ur-raq*, *mu-ru-qu* (with omission of *-ān*).

II.C.2.1.3 With a (Proto-)guttural Consonant

had-du-tu "to renew, restore" (D infinitive of Ḥ-D-Ṯ, ↑I.d.7), *ú-sa-ap-pa-hu* (↑ I.b.6).

II.C.2.2 Verba Ultimae Infirmae

II.C.2.2.1 With a (Proto-)guttural Consonant

hadû (IV): *ú-ha-du-ú* (to ʿ-D-Y, "to detach, remove, severe", ↑I.k).

II.C.3 Š Stirps

galû (G-L-Y): NB *ú-šag-lu-šú* (Š "pret."), *ul-te-ge-li* (Š pf. "deported"), *ul-te-eg-lu* (↑I.k, both with *št* → *lt*).

II.C.4 N Stirps

N-Ṭ-L: *in-na-aṭ-ṭal* (↑I.l).

II.d *Prepositions*

ba-' (followed by DINGIR^{meš}), "by (the gods");[35] *bi-* (of *bi-i-di-ia*), "with my own hand" (in a royal inscription of Nebuchadnezzar II);[36]

la- renders the Aram. prep. *l-*, "to, for";[37] *la(-)pān* "to, in front of, from before" (NA, NB/LB, very common with a wide geographical and chronological distribution); and *la(-)qāt* (+ *elû*), "upwards ... to", are Arameo-Akkadian blends like *la-le-(e-)nu*, *la-le-en-na* (↑I.a).[38]

35 Jursa 2012, 380–381.

36 CAD B: 223; Abraham and Sokoloff 2011, 28b:28.

37 Abraham and Sokoloff 2011, 38–39:116.

38 Found in correspondence from Babylon, Nippur and the Sealand, ca. Esarhaddon; Reynolds 2003, 185; and in the Rē'i-alpe archive from Borsippa, early Achaemenid; Hackl et al. 2014, 403.

III Documentary Distribution

III.a *Hapax Legomena (Partially* ad hoc *Borrowings?)*

ak-ka-di-ia (↑I.c.1), *ak-ta-ra-'* (↑I.l, II.c.1.1.4), *ak-te-ra-ma* (↑I.l, II.c.1.1.2), *a-lu-ú* (↑I.d.7), *aq-qa-bu-ú* (↑I.b.5), *a-ra* (↑0), *ba-'*, *bi-i-di-ia* (↑II.d), *dar-gu* (↑I.d.7), *ek/ik-bi* (↑I.f), *ga-lu-tu* (↑I.k), *ge-ṭi-pi* (↑I.b.6), *gu-da-nu* (↑I.d.2), *gu-ub-ba-a-ni* (↑I.j), *gu-ub-ba-tu*$_4$ (↑I.d.6), *ha-ár-ku* (↑I.g, II.c.1.1.4), *had-du-tu* (↑I.d.7), *ha-*DI-ID (↑I.d.4), *hal-la* (↑I.b.5), *ha-pa-ap* (↑II.c.1.4), ^{uzu}*hat-ti-ik* (↑I.c.2), *he-si-il-ti* (↑I.c.1), *he-šá-ru-ú* (↑I.e), *hi-iṣ* (↑I.e), *hu-ši-ni*(-šú, ↑I.l), *ia-a-qu-qa-nu*^{sar}, *ia-ar-qa-nu*^{sar} (↑I.b.2), ^{ú}*ia-bu-ṭu* (↑I.b.4), *ia-hi-il-ti* (↑ I.c.1), *in-na-aṭ-ṭal* (↑I.l), *i-se-li-iq-qu* (↑I.j, II.c.1.1.2), ^{giš}*ka-su-u* (↑I.d.6), *ke/qé-ši-ir-tu*$_4$ (↑I.b.1), *ku-ú-zu* (↑I.d.5), *lip-ra-aq* (II.c.1.1.2), *ma-as-tar* (↑I.d.7), ^{lú}*ma-gal-la-a* (↑I.a), *man-ṭa-ri* (↑I.b.3), *ni-ir-ki-il-ma* (↑I.e, II.c.1.1.3), *nu-qu-pu-tu* (↑I.b.6), *pi-ir-qú-ti*(*-šú-nu*, ↑I.f), *qa-ad-ru* (↑I.d.5), *qa-as-bi* (↑I.b.3), *qatu* (↑I.g), *qé-ši-šú* (↑I.h), *sa-ar-ri-ih* (↑I.d.3), ^{f}*sa-gi-it-tu*$_4$, *sa-git-tú* (in the same text, ↑I.i), *ṣu-ur-bi*^{sar} (I.b.2), *šá-ma-ka-a-ta* (↑I.b.4), *sul-lam-mat* (↑I.b.1), *ú-ha-du-ú* (↑I.k, II.c.2.2.1), ^{uzu}*un-qu* (↑I.c.2), *zi-ip-tu*$_4$ (↑I.d.1), *zu-up-ri-né-e* (↑I.d.2), *zu-ú-pu*^{sar} (↑I.b.2).

III.b *Dis Legomena*

gu-mat/*gu-ma-ti* (↑I.j), *kap-pi* (↑I.e), *ma-ṣi-hi* (↑I.j), *pu-ru-uh-li-ib-nu* (↑I.b.1), *ra-qu-un-du, raq-qu-*[*un-du*] (↑I.d.4), *sa-pan/pa-an* (↑I.b.1), *su-ru-u* (↑I.b.3), *še-ru-ú, iš-te-ri* (↑I.c.2, II.c.1.4.1).

The remaining lexemes have multiple occurrences.

IV Evaluation and Conclusions

IV.a *A Sociohistorical Overview*

When we view the genres of sources, we see that most lexemes are recorded in economic texts.[39] Only sixteen are recorded in non-economic documents, as such lexical (3: 7, 101; and 69 in Uruanna), medical (5: 104, 113, 135, 170, 174), and literary (1: 177). Two lexemes are recorded in both lexical and medical (167) or in both medical and literary texts (109).

Another five lexemes are datable because they occur in royal inscriptions (11a, 138) and chronicles (25a) or in texts which were found *in situ* (61, 78 in literary-religious texts, the former also in a medical text).

39 The figures in the discussion refer to Table 1, found in the online drive; see note 1.

Literary-religious texts and royal inscriptions were composed in a highly literary style. The Babylonian scribes who followed a tradition of composing literary Akkadian (i.e., Standard Babylonian) deliberately abstained from including non-Akkadian words in these texts and filtered out Aramaic terms. Exceptionally, royal inscriptions from Sūhu contain several Aramaic loanwords from as early as the mid-8th century BC. This is because Sūhu was an Aramaic-speaking region with an Amorite substrate, where Akkadian had always been merely a literary language.[40]

Another exception is the Babylonian section of the Bisutun inscription of Darius I, as well as the inscriptions of his successors. These royal inscriptions were composed in Late Babylonian, unlike the Neo-Babylonian royal inscriptions (including those of Cyrus) which were in Standard Babylonian. It was suggested that this innovative and deviating practice was motivated by the Achaemenid political aspiration to distance themselves from the literary languages of their Neo-Babylonian predecessors[41] Only the Teispid Cyrus left a meagre corpus, which was still composed in the tradition of the Neo-Babylonian royal inscriptions.

In my opinion, the main reason for this shift was practical. Darius I and his advisors realized that their propaganda can be widely intelligible and absorbable by using the vernacular. Therefore, one encounters several Aramaic words there (it is suspected that the LB version was influenced by the Aramaic version of the Bisutun inscription). The Babylonian version of the Bisutun trilingual (or quadrilingual if the Aramaic version is added) contains elaborations on Babylonian events. On the contrary, the cylinder inscription of Antiochus I Soter is in Standard Babylonian and even after a gap of almost 250 years, still strictly adheres to the puristic tradition of the Neo-Babylonian royal inscriptions.

The scribes of the practical texts had to adapt themselves to some extent to the bilingual milieu of Babylonia in the age of empires, when the countryside of the alluvium was inhabited mainly by Arameo-Chaldeans (both Arameophones) and the urban centres, whose citizens were the main bearers of the Akkadian culture. These were flooded by several waves of mainly Levantine deportees and prisoners of war. These deportees were mostly speakers of Aramaic and cognate West Semitic dialects.

Regarding the heterogeneous group of Neo-Babylonian/Late Babylonian practical texts, the legal deeds which consist primarily of traditional formularies contain much less foreign lexemes than the less formal administrative

40 For words with Amorite forerunners, see IOS 22, Part 1, Introduction; add *ma-di-na-at*, discussed by van der Spek 2015.

41 Beaulieu 2006, 204.

records. In addition, the deeds were written mostly for urbanite Babylonians. In most cases both parties to the transactions belonged to this indigenous and segregate group. An exception are the dialogue contracts, especially from the late Achaemenid period, and notably from the Murašû archive, which contain more Aramaic loanwords.

The records and the letters also have some Aramaic loanwords. Administrative lists and other such records are basically ephemeral and have practical purposes. Therefore, they list words which were in current use among the Arameo-Chaldean employees of the palatial and temple sector. Likewise, Aramaic lexemes are more often found in lists of realia and commodities that are embedded in deeds and letters.[42] Letters from the eastern periphery of the alluvium near the Tigris, which was the abode of Aramean tribes, as well as the dossier of Bēl-ibni from southern Babylonia, contain Aramaic military, communication and other terms such as *ṭùl-lu-um-ma-'-u*, "injustice" (referring to the adversaries, ↑I.f), as well as *mâru*, "to buy; to procure food" and its derivative *mi-i-ri*, "food, sustenance", procured from the Aramean tribe of Puqūdu. Both terms occur in a peculiar context. The sender spontaneously describes his enemies in an unrestrained expression of his vernacular.

A document from Uruk dated to 27.IX.0 Cambyses = 529 BC allows a glimpse at the use of Aramaic in the countryside. A functionary of Eanna ordered an alphabet scribe to write a letter to the commissioner (*bēl-piqitti*) of the rural settlement Ālu-ša-Kī-Nabû.[43] A certain Aplâ s. of Sîn-aha-iddina, who possessed an Aramaic sealed document, was based or at least was active in the rural settlement Hurbat-Kalbi in 536 BC according to a deed from the Eanna archive.[44]

IV.b *Chronological Distribution*

In this section, we provide an overview of the chronological distribution of the loadwords. Overall, the largest concentration of Aramaic loanwords is in the long 6th century BC, simply because most of the documentation is from this period. The second largest is the Sargonid period, followed by the late Achaemenid and Hellenistic-Parthian, and the post-Kassite period, when only eight Aramaic lexemes are recorded in Babylonia proper, since this was the initial stage of the Chaldeo-Aramean penetration to the alluvium.

Here by follows a break-down of the lexemes according to their chronological distribution.

42 Cf., e.g., TCL 9, 117 = Levavi 2018, 156.

43 YOS 7, 102; Bloch 2018, 52–57.

44 YOS 7, 19; Bloch 2018, 57–59.

Twelve lexemes (9.3 %), which are not recorded in practical texts, can at best be datable to the 1st millennium BC, but not to a specific period.[45]

Post-Kassite period (c. 850–723 BC) has eleven lexemes (7.75 %), including three from Sūhu, and two from Nippur, viz. 9, 72, 118 and 80, 110, respectively, referring to an Aramaic-speaking region outside Babylonia and to a segment of the Chaldeo-Aramean countryside. Three are recorded later (124 also Sargonid, 14 and 84 as late as the Achaemenid and Hellenistic period); 90, 132, 162.

Sargonid period (722–627 BC) has 18 (13.95 %),[46] plus 14 which are also recorded in the long 6th century BC;[47] two occurring also in the late-Achaemenid period (71, 88) and one in the Hellenistic period (2).

The long 6th century BC (626–484 BC) includes 79 (61.24 %),[48] plus five, which are also recorded in the late Achaemenid period (33, 42, 75, 129, 137), and another five (47, 100, 123, 141, 172), which occur also in the Hellenistic-Parthian period. One lexeme (179) is recorded in an unpublished text, whose date and type are not reported. It is labelled as "spB", in which case it is datable to the long 6th century BC or to the Achaemenid or Hellenistic-Parthian periods.

The late Achaemenid period (483–332 BC) has 11 lexemes (8.52 %).[49] Two lexemes are either late Achaemenid or early Hellenistic (3, 85) and three are recorded both in the late Achaemenid and Hellenistic-Parthian periods (61, 78, 85). The Hellenistic-Parthian period (331 BC–75 CE) has 11 lexemes (8.52 %).[50]

IV.c *Geographic Distribution*

On the whole, it should be remembered that both the chronological and geographical distribution of the Aramaic loanwords are dictated by the general NB/LB documentation, which is very scanty during the post-Kassite period, sparse and non-variagated in the ensuing Sargonid period and reaches its peak during the long 6th century. It shrinks from the late Achaemenid period onwards. This documentation stems mostly from the urban centres, mainly from their temple archives (notably the Eanna and the Ebabbar), as well as from

45 1st millennium: 7, 15, 69, 101, 104, 109, 113, 135, 167, 170, 174, 177.

46 Sargonid: 6, 25, 39, 41, 60, 64, 67, 68, 96, 106, 107, 134, 142, 152, 161, 168, 175, 180.

47 Lexemes continuing into the long 6th century: 13, 21, 24, 38, 55, 83, 87, 97, 102, 126, 139, 146, 159, 171.

48 Long 6th century BC: 1, 5, 8, 10–12, 18–20, 22, 23, 26–32, 34, 35, 37, 43–46, 48, 49, 51, 54, 57, 58, 65, 66, 70, 73, 74, 76, 79, 81, 82, 89, 95, 103, 105, 111, 112, 114–117, 119–121, 127, 130, 131, 136, 138, 143–145, 147–149, 151, 153–158, 160, 163, 166, 169, 173, 176, 178.

49 Late Achaemenid: 36, 40, 56, 62, 86, 92, 99, 108, 128, 133, 164.

50 Hellenistic-Parthian: 4, 17, 50, 53, 59, 77, 91, 93, 122, 125, 150.

private archives of urban families and later on (after the long 6th century BC) of private entrepreneurs of more humble extraction.

The majority of the documentation (78 = 60.45 %) comes from Sippar (32 = 24.8 %) and Uruk (46 = 35.65 %). Nippur lags far behind (11 = 8.52 %). The southern and eastern periphery, as well as Sūhu, reach 13.55–15.5 % (16–20 lexemes).

The survey of geographical distribution proceeds from north to south.

Sippar: 6.[51] Nine more lexemes are recorded in Sippar and other places.[52] More material is implicitly from Sippar, as it is recorded in the archive of its main temple, the Ebabbar.[53] One lexeme (57) is from Āl-Šamaš in the region of Sippar.

Babylon: 27.[54] Ten more lexemes are recorded in Babylon and other places.[55] One lexeme (3) is perhaps from Cutha and two are from Kish (164 and 144 which is also recorded in Sippar).

Borsippa: 11, including one which was issued in Sippar but belongs to a Borsippean archive (114).[56] Three more lexemes are recorded in Borsippa and other places.[57]

Two lexemes are from the Babylonian isthmus (85; 76 is recorded in Sippar and Uruk as well) and another two in central Babylonia (13, 88; 25, 39, 108 and 126 are recorded also elsewhere).

Nippur: 13.[58] Eight more lexemes are recorded in Nippur and other places.[59]

Uruk: 16.[60] Thirteen more lexemes are recorded in Uruk and other places.[61]

---

51 Sippar: 19, 54, 103, 130, 151, 155.

52 Sippar and other places: 21 (Babylon), 22 (Babylon, Uruk), 48 (Babylon, Dilbat, Uruk), 76 (Babylonian isthmus, Uruk), 83, 119, 149 (Uruk), 144 (Kish), 171 (Tupliyaš).

53 Ebabbar: 45, 51, 79, 111, 115, 160, 163, 173, 178; the Ebabbar and the Eanna temple of Uruk: 30, 46, 74, 105, 147, 154.

54 Babylon: 8, 16, 18, 23, 28, 29, 59, 64–68, 77, 93, 106, 107, 125, 129, 137, 138, 150, 152, 158, 161, 172, 175, 180.

55 Babylon and other places: 11 (Borsippa), 21 (Sippar), 22 (Sippar, Uruk), 35 (Nippur), 39 (central Babylonia, southern Babylonia, Uruk), 47, 74 (Uruk), 48 (Sippar, Dilbat, Uruk), 88a (Borsippa, Nippur, Sealand) and 82 (Opis).

56 Borsippa: 5, 21a, 32, 55, 58, 115, 117, 127, 143, 177.

57 Borsippa and other places: 11 (Babylon), 88a (Babylon, Nippur, Sealand) and 92 (Nippur).

58 Nippur: 33, 36, 40, 42, 56, 62, 80, 86, 99, 110, 128, 133, 156.

59 Nippur and other places: 35 (Babylon), 52 (Uruk), 75 (Bīt-Našar, Bīt-Dakkūru, Uruk), 88a (Babylon, Borsippa, Sealand), 92 (Borsippa), 100 (Uruk, Ur), 108 (central Babylonia, Uruk), 126 (central Babylonia).

60 Uruk: 4, 17, 50, 53, 60, 61, 73, 78, 91, 112, 122, 123, 131, 136, 139, 145.

61 Uruk and other places: 22 (Sippar, Babylon), 25 (central Babylonia), 47 (Babylon), 48 (Sippar, Babylon, Dilbat), 52 (Nippur), 74 (Babylon), 75 (Nippur, Bīt-Našar, Bīt-Dakkūru), 76 (Sippar, Babylonian isthmus), 83, 119, 149 (Sippar), 100 (Nippur, Ur), 108 (central Babylonia, Nippur).

More material is implicitly from Uruk, as it is recorded in the archive of the main temple of Uruk, the Eanna, with 16 lexemes.[62] Four more occur both in the archive of the Eanna and that of the Ebabbar temple (30, 46, 105, 147). One more lexeme (89) is from the Uruk region.

Ur: two lexemes, which are also recorded elsewhere, 94 (Birāti, eastern Babylonia) and 100 (Nippur, Uruk).

Two lexemes are from southern Babylonia (96, 168).

The Chaldean territories have one common lexeme (124), Bīt-Awkānu has two (38, 97) and Bīt-Dakkūru two (95 from Dūru-ša-Bīt-Dakkūru; 75 is also recorded in Bīt-Našar, Nippur and Uruk).

The Sealand has three lexemes (41, 134; 146 recurs in Tupliyaš). Tupliyaš has two lexemes which are also recorded in the Sealand (146) and Sippar (171). Sūhu (outside Babylonia, an Aramaic-speaking region) has three lexemes (9, 72, 118).

IV.d *The Loanwords According to the Parts of Speech*

The material in question follows universal distributional patterns, conforming to the general tendencies of borrowing foreign lexical material. The overwhelming majority of the Aramaic loanwords in Neo-Babylonian/Late Babylonian are substantives, numbered at 126.[63] This includes substantivized adjectives (originally passive participles), like *ga-bi-bi, ha-ṭi-ṭi, gam-mi-da-tu$_4$, hat-ti-ik, ge-ṭi-pi* and *he-si-il-ti,* (18, 22, 26, 28, 54, 55, 57), active participles (*ia-a-ri-tu$_4$, sa-gi-it-tu$_4$,* and *se-pi-ru,* 65, 131, 141) and other nominal forms of the verbal system, viz. *ha-ár-ku* (41), *had-du-tu* (43), *su-ub-bu-su-tu* (146), as well as the infinitives *a-pu-ú* (5) and *ha-pa-ap* (51); this is altogether 138 (out of 180 = 76.66 %).

Non-substantivized adjectives are very few (*a-lu-ú,* 4 and *ta-am-mi-im,* fem. *ta-mì-mi-tu$_4$,* 164). This is compatible with linguistic universals, namely, that substantives unlike verbs are easily borrowed. Consequently, the number of verbs lag far behind. It is only 26 (14.44 %).[64]

Pronouns are very rare. Only the proximal demonstrative *a-ga-a* (2) and the interrogative pronoun *ki-ma-'* (83) are documented. The former did not entirely suppress Akkad. *annû,* "this". In addition, Aramaic probably triggered

62 The Eanna: 20, 26, 27, 34, 38, 43, 44, 49, 70, 81, 120, 121, 148, 153, 157, 169.

63 Substantives: 1, 3, 6–10, 14–17, 19–24, 27, 29–40, 42, 44–50, 52, 53, 56, 58, 59, 61–64, 66, 67, 69, 70, 74–77, 79, 81, 82, 84, 85, 87, 90–95, 97–99, 101–103, 108, 112–117, 119–121, 123–125, 128–130, 133, 135, 137, 141–145, 147–158, 161, 166–180.

64 Verbs: 13, 25, 60, 68. 71–73, 78, 80, 89, 96, 100, 107, 109, 110, 118, 122, 126, 127, 132, 136, 138–140, 159, 160.

the emergence in Neo-Babylonian/Late Babylonian of the form *anīnu*, "we", which replaced the form *nīnu*.[65]

There are only two prepositions (13, 88) and just one adverb (86). Again, this is not surprising, seeing that pronouns, adverbs and particles are universally almost blocked to borrowing.

IV.e *Distribution by Semantic-Topical Groups*

Here are the categories in descending order (I.a-l): Flora and material culture: 23.21 % each; behaviour and human condition, as well as commerce, fiscal terms, taxation and measurements: 7.73 % each; fauna: 7.14 %; legal, customary and moral terms, as well as topography and climate: 5.95 % each; social status and organization: 4.76 %; writing: 4.16 %; military terms and occupations-offices: 3.57 % each; transportation, movement and communication: 2.97 %.

IV.f *Discussion*

The period from *c.* 900 to 100 BC, an *ad hoc* chronological framework, which is dictated by the available cuneiform documentation, must have been that of an extended linguistic symbiosis between Akkadian and Aramaic.[66] It stands to reason that the degree of linguistic interference or, in a more figurative sense, linguistic osmosis varied to some extent within this long period of 800 years.

Generally, it would be reasonable to envisage that the later the date within this period, the more intensive the interference, with the linguistic osmosis more intensive and accelerated in the periphery of the Babylonian alluvial plain and in the countryside. There must have been an ever-increasing tension between the conservative and puristic tendencies of the Babylonian scribes, whose thorough training in the *Edubba* enabled them to write literary and idiomatic Akkadian and the ever-increasing number of speakers of the Aramaic vernacular.[67]

The urbanites' ingrained conservatism and loyalty to the Akkadian language was explicitly shared by Sargon II. This can be highlighted by a comparison of the lexical content of royal Sargonid letters sent to Babylonia, which is almost devoid of Aramaic loanwords, with that of the contemporary correspondence from southern and eastern Babylonia, where such loanwords are not rare. These tendencies combined with the official encouragement should be taken into account when one assesses the preservation forces of the indigenous

65 Beaulieu 2013, 362–365.

66 The term was coined by Greenfield 1995, 17.

67 Beaulieu 2013.

language, Akkadian, which served as the sole vehicle of written communication in Mesopotamia for almost a millennium after the demise of Sumerian.[68] However, we should note that the scribes of archival documents were under constant compulsions of adapting themselves to the needs of the non-urban listees of administrative records and the ethno-lingistically diverse parties of legal deeds. The verbal blend *ibi-inna* (↑II.C.1.6) is a vivid reminiscence of an encounter between such parties.

The main difficulty for the topic under discussion—the identification of population groups from the implicit evidence—is the tension between the persistent Akkadian scribal tradition and the surrounding vernaculars. The strict and meticulous upbringing of the Babylonian scribes in the Sumero-Akkadian scholarly tradition, their adherence to legal formularies, patterns of administrative documents, and epistolographic practices, form a tight mask, in fact an almost hermetic seal, against the changing linguistic environment. The scribes' resistence to change (at least from external influences) must be recognized as the centrepoint of the problem of Akkadian-Aramaic linguistic interference, where the factors behind the affected semantic fields remain to be clarified.

At this juncture it should be considered whether the borrowings from Aramaic were motivated by the need to fill a lexical void in Akkadian. It seems to me that such a void was minimal: I listed in Table 1 (and see note 1), at least 119 contemporary Akkadian (NB/LB and SB from *c.* 900–200 BC) words which are *grosso modo* the equivalents of Aramaic loanwords. Most of them naturally belong to the realm of realia. The fact that the abundant Neo-Babylonian/Late Babylonian corpus from this long period contains no more than 180 Aramaic loanwords is the crown witness of the successful resistance of the conservative Akkadian scribes.

Out of at least 97 Akkadian equivalents of the Aramaic loanwords, at least 14 are cognates.[69] The majority (at least nine) are minimal pairs, which may have been the result of a certain degree of convergence.[70]

Cases of integration are three words (13a, 109a and 165), which have an Aramaic derivation, but are formed according to an Akkadian nominal pattern.

68 An analogous case of preservation forces can be detected in Middle Hebrew vs Western Aramaic, which like Akkadian and (the precursor of) Eastern Aramaic, are cognate languages; see Gluska 1999, 117–118.

69 Aramaic loanwords: 2, 4, 5, 7, 8, 11, 13–15, 17, 19–21, 23, 25, 27, 28–33, 36, 38, 39, 43, 44, 46, 47, 49, 51, 54, 55, 57–61, 68, 71, 73, 76, 78, 80, 83, 84, 87–90, 94, 96, 97, 101, 104, 106, 108–111, 116, 118–120, 122, 124–127, 130, 132–134, 136–139, 145–147, 153, 154, 156–160, 162, 164–166, 168–172, 174, 175, 178; Cognates: 4, 5, 7, 8, 13, 14, 28, 36, 43, 89, 108, 124, 125, 170, 172 and perhaps 116. For selected cases of cognate loanwords, see Beaulieu 2013, 371–374.

70 Minimal pairs: 4, 5, 8, 13, 89, 108, 124, 170, 172.

Like other loanwords, the Aramaic lexemes recorded in Neo-Babylonian/Late Babylonian texts have generally the Akkadian plural suffix, when they refer to multiple items. Two lexemes have the same form both in Akkadian and Aramaic, but their semantic range differs (14, 16). A case of a calque is seen in 13.[71]

In Neo-Babylonian/Late Babylonian texts, the terms referring to writing in Aramaic and the inscribed media, notably parchment and stone, as well as the professional title of the alphabet scribe are Aramaic. The universal principle that the lexemes come together with the imported objects and techniques applies here as well.

Non-endemic plants (the largest group), imported commodities, as well as newly introduced tools and containers bear non-Akkadian, mostly Aramaic, names. Certain containers were in use in international trade. Therefore, the large storage vessel mostly containing imported wine, is an Aramaic loanword of Levantine origin (*kandu*, possibly ultimately Phoenician, has a geographical distribution both east and west of Phoenicia, 76). There is some reason to suspect that *sa-pi-na-tu*$_4$ "big boat, ship" (↑1.k), i.e., a vessel capable for carrying bulk, originates from Levantine Aramaic (and ultimately from Phoenician?).

Akkadian borrowed not only terms which reflect advanced technology, but also words denoting basic utensils used by (semi-)nomads, such as **gūdu* and *nūṭu*, referring to leather bottles, which were used by Babylonian soldiers (↑1.d.2), as they were more suitable for field conditions than the Babylonian standard bottles (Akkad. *lahannu*, pre-NB) made of clay, glass or metal.

Plants in the garden of Merodach-baladan II, a Chaldean king of Babylonia, bear Aramaic names (↑1.b.2). The by-products of dates (1.b.3) were obtained from the gardeners, who generally did not belong to the urban elite, who were the bearers of Akkadian culture. Many palm groves were located in the Chaldean territories and it may be surmised that the Chaldeans specialized in the cultivation of the date palm. The Chaldeo-Arameans had a significant share of this cultivation in the 1st millennium BC.

The agricultural operations (↑1.b.6: *sippihu, nuqupūtu*) and their results (*geṭīpu*) were conducted by cultivators and gardeners who were generally non-urban. This may point to a lexical pressure from below. The other plants include at least two dendronyms whose origin must have been outside Mesopotamia, *šam/nṭu* (← Egyptian, ↑1.b.4) and *sa-ap-al-gi-nu* (probably non-Semitic, ↑0). They entered the Babylonian record via Aramaic. *Qunnabu* "cannabis" is an exception. The name is arguably Aramaic, although the plant is not endemic to the Middle East. It seems that it was coined upon its introduction and was

71 For another case, see Hackl 2021a, 1444.

originally a general term denoting "trimmings of herbs". Intrestingly enough, the designation of "hemp" in Sanskrit, a language spoken in the area where hemp originated, has a similar meaning, "breaking" (of hemp).

Since the countryside has become overwhelmingly Aramaic-speaking, one encounters several Aramaic topographical terms referring mostly to the agricultural landscape. The only loanword with a climatic denotation refers to seasonal crops.

The second-largest group of loans is material culture. Regarding minerals, the main source of bitumen was Hīt in the Aramaic-speaking region of Sūhu. Lists of fabrics and house utensils are mostly found in dowry contracts. Such lists of realia, which are partially in another language than that of the deed itself, are a universal phenomenon in multilingual environments. These words generally originate from the vernacular.[72]

Aramaic loanwords referring to textiles generally do not denote prestige garments; none of them had a sacral usage, except for *uzāru*.

The invention of iron tools and their introduction to the labour market was a process that slowly took place mainly during the Iron Age II, when the Arameo-Chaldeans became an important pool of workmen in the Babylonian palatial and temple sectors. Implements are generally listed in administrative records. Earthenware, stoneware and reed basketry belong to the basic inventory of the lower classes, who also produced them. Basketry was a typical occupation of low-class women.

Reed cutters, JBA *qṭyl qny(')* (sg.), were always considered one of the least prestigious jobs in Babylonia.[73] The fishing nets bear an Aramaic term (133). Why is this so? The first reason is the lack of an exact equivalent for this implement in Neo-Babylonian/Late Babylonian, and second is the recipients of this means of production. In the few recorded cases we have, they were probably non-indigenous.

None of the Aramaic terms of constructions and edifices denote a sacred or holy structure. Typically, one of them, which occurs in a peripheral-rural archive, refers to shelter for livestock (90). An Aramaic term for canal and of a storehouse (↑1.d.7) were used along with the rich Akkadian vocabulary for man-made waterways and storage facilities.

Regarding fauna (↑1.c), several designations of domestic animals, both cattle and small stock, as well as those of meat cuts, are Aramaic. This is due to the

72 Cf., e.g., the Arabic (partially ← Iranian and Greek) designations of realia which are included in Aramaic *ketubba* documents from Medieval Palestine and Egypt; Friedman 1981, 138, 145–146, 186, 189, 286–287.

73 Sokoloff 2020, 981b, 1004–1005 *ad* BT San. 82b (28).

considerable presence of Chaldeo-Arameans in animal husbandry. It may be suspected that these terms, which partially replaced age-long Akkadian terms, stem from the pastoralists' sociolect.

Shepherds are generally also experts of preparing milk products, such as cheese and yoghurt. No wonder that the Aramaic term *gubnatu* (Aram. *gubnā*), "cheese made of sheep milk", which was recorded in Achaemenid Babylonia, suppressed the original Akkadian term, which was *eqīdu*.

Animal husbandry supplied raw material for the leather industry, hence two lexemes denoting "leather" are originally Aramaic. "Shears, clippers for shearing" (*si-ir-pi/pu*, ↑1.d.4) may also have been coined by shepherds. Perhaps also the unattested singular of *ṣuppātu* "strips of carded wool" or "braided curtains" (↑1.d.3) is originally a *nomen unitatis* of the general term for "wool", current among Arameo-Arabian shepherds of small stock, who were the suppliers of the raw material.

The Neo-Babylonian legal terminology borrowed *adû* in the Sargonid period, when several words used by the Assyrian administration were adopted by the Babylonians. In the sphere of international law, this word is initially recorded as "treaty, covenant". In Babylonia it is generally followed by the name of the current ruler in assertory oaths, mostly in deeds of the temple and private sectors.

Legal terms of the private sphere, such as *murruqu* "clear from claims" and *harara/harhara* "objection, protest" (to a legal decision), began to be used later (in the long 6th century BC and the late Achaemenid period respectively).

The taxation practice of *ka-an-šú* was in force already in the Neo-Babylonian empire, while *ušrû* (← Aram.) is a by-form of Akkad. *ešrû* "tithe", but it did not entirely suppress the Akkadian cognate. The *haṭru*-organization whose main purpose was to facilitate taxation has a compact documentation in the late Achaemenid period, but it may have had earlier roots. The loss of independence and the ensuing transformation of Babylonia into a province within the much wider Achaemenid imperial framework, where Aramaic served as the *lingua franca*, brought with it a certain degree of standardization of the monetary and taxation systems, as well as of the legal practice. Hence Aramaic commercial, fiscal means (coins), and transportation terms were introduced.

Another term borrowed from the *lingua franca* is *ma-di-na-at* "satrapy" (see p. 80, n. 40). Regarding *šelû*, one has to reckon here with code-switching: warnings, like curses, were written in the vernacular. The warnings and curses were intended, in the first place, to alert the local population in their own language.[74]

74 Jursa 2012, 380.

The isolated occurrence of *bi-*, viz., in *bi-i-di-ia* "with my own hand" (cf. *yad*, ↑I.e) is a case of code switching, which is not surprising given the ruler's Chaldean extraction.

Since Aramaic had not yet replaced Akkadian as *the* official and prestigious language during the period of the Neo-Babylonian empire, there are almost no Aramaic terms for offices. The term *paqūdu*, referring to a municipal official, interchanges with its Akkadian cognates, such as *paqdu*. In this semantic category with its inherited vocabulary, there was no niche for lexical innovations. The only Aramaic terms referring to offices, such as Chaldean and Aramean chieftains, are not recorded after the loss of Babylonian independence. The hapax *qé-ši-šú* (↑I.h) is merely honorific. On the other hand, several Aramaic loanwords refer to people of low status (*lawwūtānu* and *halpu*, ↑I.h), non-prestigious occupations and one functionary of non-institutional religion. This served the needs of the organization of labour. Paradoxically, *kiništu*, the term for an assembly of the temple, the stronghold of Babylonian culture and particularism, is Aramaic. It is recorded throughout the 1st millennium. Likewise, *šīhu* refers almost exclusively to temple land. Both loanwords entered Akkadian before 750 BC, when the shutters were pulled down and seclusion and endogamy became the norm among the Babylonian urbanites.

Regarding the consolidation of the borrowings, it is not always possible to establish which of them were fluctuant, i.e., with a low degree of absorption. The 31 Aramaic loanwords which show continuity, i.e., are recorded in more than one period, can be regarded as having a high degree of absorption.[75] It is noteworthy that loans, which are recorded only in lexical lists and literary texts, are not necessarily of low degree of absorption. Their degree varies from case to case. On the whole, there must have been external pressures and accelerated internationalization, especially from the Achaemenid period onwards, as well as internal compulsions caused mainly by the spread of Aramaic as the *lingua franca* of the age of empires, which had reached its maximum territorial diffusion during the Achaemenid period.

The Achaemenid period also witnessed the presence of the alphabet (Aramaic) scribes in every sector, institution and settlement of a significant size and/or location.[76] It should be remembered that the practice of writing in Aramaic in Babylonia was in all probability promulgated by the Sargonids. No wonder that individuals of Assyrian extraction are later recorded among the

75 Aramaic loanwords with continuity: 2, 13, 14, 21, 24, 33, 38, 42, 47, 55, 71, 75, 78, 83, 84, 87, 88, 97, 100, 102, 123, 124, 126, 129, 137, 139, 141, 146, 159, 171, 172.

76 Bloch 2018.

alphabet scribes.[77] The economic activity, notably commerce, met with minimal social resistance by the dwindling and weakened Babylonian elite. There was an effective and utilitarian use of the vernacular for day-to-day communication and negotiation. It can be envisaged that in the terminal stage of its usage Akkadian had become merely a *lingua sacra*.[78]

Two additional points are to be addressed in this conclusion.

Morphological interference is extant, e.g., in the plural. LB *un-qu-a-tú*/NA *un-qu-a-ti* (PBS 2/1, 185, 4 and CT 53, 904, 3′) for *unqāti* and *qul-mu-a-te* render ← Aram. fem. pl. *-wt*, like NA *qa-nu-a-te* "reeds", whose base is not identical with Aram. **qany-* ← **qanay*.[79]

The broken pl. ^{gada}*gi-da-lu-ú* is also due to Aramaic interference.[80] There was also a certain degree of convergence in the verbal system due to Aramaic interference.[81] The plural suffix *-īyā* originates from Aram. *-ayyā*.[82]

Regarding semantics and lexicon, we can add that due to specialization there is an impressive variety of terms referring to the date palm and its products both in Eastern Aramaic and in Akkadian. This phenomenon is an application of the famous observations of Levi-Strauss which has become an anthropological universal. For instance, Akkadian has an extensive terminology of containers made of earthenware and reeds, and shares with Aramaic a rich lexical inventory for various species of locust.[83]

References

Abraham, Kathleen and Michael Sokoloff. 2011. "Aramaic Loanwords in Akkadian—A Reassessment of the Proposals." *AfO* 51: 22–76.

Amar, Zohar. 2004. *The Locust in Jewish Tradition.* (in Hebrew). Ramat-Gan: Bar-Ilan University.

77 E.g., Mukīn-zēri s. of Ardaššu in Sippar, Ebabbar archive, 573 BC; Bloch 2018, 109–113:21. The last witness is an Assyrian, who is preceded by witnesses bearing surnames. This is probably a ranked list, therefore, in this case there is no need to regard the gentilic "Assyrian" as a surname. And Pān-Iššār-lūmur of the crown prince's household, 523 BC; Bloch 2018, 140–142:35.

78 For the death of Akkadian as a spoken language, see Hackl 2021b, 1459–1469.

79 CAD U/W: 167, 171; CAD Q: 300a, s.v. *qulmû*, e (82-7-14, 1473, 2, unpubl.); Zadok 1997; cf. Cherry 2017, 216–217.

80 Bloch 2018, 135, n. 91.

81 Beaulieu 2013, 365–371.

82 Hackl 2021a, 1450.

83 CAD E: 256–258; Bodenheimer 1949, 174–178; Amar 2004, 105–118.

Aro, Jussi. 1964. *Die Vokalisierung des Grundstammes im semitischen Verbum*. StOr 31. Helsinki: Academia scientiarum Fennica.

Avi-Yonah, Michael. 1976. *Gazetteer of Roman Palestine*. Qedem 5. Jerusalem: Carta.

Bar-Asher Siegal. 2016. *Introduction to the Grammar of Jewish Babylonian Aramaic*. LOS III: Aramaic, 3. 2nd Revised and Extended Ed. Münster: Ugarit Verlag.

Beaulieu, Paul-Alain. 2006. "Official and Vernacular Languages: The Shifting Sands of Imperial and Cultural Identities in First-Millennium B.C. Mesopotamia." In *Margins of Writing, Origins of Cultures*. Oriental Institute Seminars 2, edited by Seth Sanders, 187–216. Chicago: Oriental Institute.

Beaulieu, Paul-Alain. 2013. "Aspects of Aramaic and Babylonian Linguistic Interaction in First Millennium BC Iraq." *Journal of Language Contact* 6: 358–378.

Beyer, Klaus. 1984. *Die aramäischen Texte vom Toten Meer samt den Inschriften aus Palästina, dem Testament Levis aus der Kairoer Genisa, der Fastenrolle und den alten talmudischen Zitaten* 1, 2. Göttingen: Vandenhoeck & Ruprecht.

Beyer, Klaus. 1994. *Die aramäischen Texte vom Toten Meer samt den Inschriften aus Palästina, dem Testament Levis aus der Kairoer Genisa, der Fastenrolle und den alten talmudischen Zitaten. Ergänzugsband*. Göttingen: Vandenhoeck & Ruprecht.

Bloch, Yigal. 2018. *Alphabetic Scribes in the Land of Cuneiform: Sēpiru Professionals in Mesopotamia in the Neo-Babylonian and Achaemenid Periods*. Piscataway: Gorgias.

Bodenheimer, Shimon. 1949. *Animal Life in Biblical Lands*. (in Hebrew). Jerusalem: Mosad Bialik.

Bravmann, Meir Moshe. 1977. *Studies in Semitic Philology*. Leiden: Brill.

Brockelmann, Carl. 1908. *Grundriss der vergleichenden Grammatik der semitischen Sprachen* 1: *Laut- und Formenlehre*. Berlin: Reimer (repr. Hildesheim: Olms, 1961).

Cherry, Zachary. 2017. *Aramaic Loanwords in Neo-Assyrian 900–600 BC*. Uppsala: Uppsala University.

Cohen, Mark Eliot. 2011. *An English to Akkadian Companion to the Assyrian Dictionaries*. Bethesda, MD: CDL.

Degen, Rainer. 1974. "Zur Bedeutung von *bgn* in den Hatra Inschriften." *NESE* 2: 99–104.

Dietrich, Manfried. 2003. *The Babylonian Correspondence of Sargon and Sennacherib*. SAA 17. Helsinki: Helsinki University.

Eilers, Wilhelm. 1936. "Eine mittelpersische Wortform aus früh-achämenidischer Zeit?" *ZDMG* 90: 160–200.

Fales, Frederick Mario. 1980. "Accadico e aramaico: livelli dell'interferenza linguistica." *Vicino Oriente* 3: 243–267.

Frame, Grant.1995. *Rulers of Babylonia from the Second Dynasty of Isin to the End of Assyrian Domination (1157–612 BC)*. RIM Babylon 2. Toronto: Toronto University.

Friedman, Mordechai Akiva. 1981. *Jewish Marriage in Palestine: A Cairo Geniza Study, 2: The Ketubba Texts*. Tel Aviv and New York: Tel Aviv University and The Jewish Theological Seminary of America.

Gluska, Isaac. 1999. *Hebrew and Aramaic in Contact During the Tannaitic Period: A Sociolinguistic Approach.* (in Hebrew). Tel Aviv: Papyrus.

Goshen-Gottstein, Moshe Henry. 1970. *A Syriac-English Glossary with Etymological Notes.* Wiesbaden: Harrassowitz.

Greenfield, Jonas Carl. 1995. "Aramaic and the Jews." In *Studia Aramaica.* JSS Supplement 4, edited by Markham J. Geller and Michael P. Weitzmann, 1–18. Oxford: Oxford University.

Gzella, Holger. 2014. "Language and Script." In *The Arameans in Ancient Syria.* HdO 1/106, edited by Herbert Niehr, 71–107. Leiden: Brill.

Hackl, Johannes, Michael Jursa, Martina Schmidl and Klaus Wagensonner 2014. *Spätbabylonische Privatbriefe.* Spätbabylonische Briefe 1. AOAT 414/1. Münster: Ugarit Verlag.

Hackl, Johannes. 2012. "Zur Funktion von (i)binni in Neu- und Spätbabylonischen." ZA 102 100–114.

Hackl, Johannes. 2021a. "Late Babylonian." In *History of the Akkadian Language, 2: The Second and First Millennia BCE, Afterlife.* HdO I 152, edited by Juan-Pablo Vita, 1431–1458. Leiden: Brill.

Hackl, Johannes. 2021b. "The Death of Akkadian as a Written and Spoken Language." In *History of the Akkadian Language, 2: The Second and First Millennia BCE, Afterlife.* HdO I 152, edited by Juan-Pablo Vita, 1459–1477. Leiden: Brill.

Hess, Christian. 2021. "(Early) Neo-Babylonian." In *History of the Akkadian Language, 2: The Second and First Millennia BCE, Afterlife.* HdO I 152, edited by Juan-Pablo Vita, 1396–1430. Leiden: Brill.

Jursa, Michael. 2012. "Ein Beamter flucht auf Aramäisch: Alphabetschreiber in der spätbabylonischen Epistolographie und die Rolle des Aramäischen in der babylonischen Verwaltung des sechsten Jahrhunderts v.Chr." In *Leggo! Studies Presented to Frederick Mario Fales on His 65th Birthday,* edited by Giovanni Battista Lanfranchi, Daniele Morandi Bonacossi, Cinzia Pappi, and Simonetta Ponchia, 380–397. Wiesbaden: Harrassowitz.

Levavi, Yuval. 2018. *Administrative Epistolography in the Formative Phase of the Neo-Babylonian Empire.* Spätbabylonische Briefe 2. Dubsar 3. Münster: Ugarit Verlag.

Müller-Kessler, Christa. 2011. "Beiträge zum Babylonisch-Talmudisch-Aramäischen Wörterbuch." *Or* 80: 214–251.

Muraoka, Takamitsu. 1976. "Segolate Nouns in Biblical and Other Aramaic Dialects." *JAOS* 96: 226–235.

Paulus, Susanne. 2014. *Die babylonischen Kudurru-Inschriften von der kassitischen bis zur frühneubabylonischen Zeit; untersucht unter besonderer Berücksichtigung gesellschafts- und rechtshistorischer Fragestellungen.* AOAT 51. Münster: Ugarit Verlag.

Payne, Elizabeth E. 2013. "Two Tablets from the Yale Babylonian Collection Mentioning the *guzguzu*-garment." *NABU* 2013: 25–27 (no. 15).

Qimron, Elisha. 1983. *Biblical Aramaic*, 2nd ed. (in Hebrew). Jerusalem: Yad Yizhak Ben-Zvi.

Reynolds, Frances. 2003. *The Babylonian Correspondence of Esarhaddon*. SAA 18. Helsinki: Helsinki University.

Sandowicz, Małgorzata. 2019. *Neo-Babylonian Dispute Documents in the British Museum*. Dubsar 11. Münster: Zaphon.

Schaeder, Hans Heinrich. 1938. "Eine verkannte aramäische Präposition." *OLZ* 41: 592–599.

von Soden, Wolfram. 1966, 1977. "Aramäische Wörter in neuassyrischen und neu- und spätbabylonischen Texte. Ein Vorbericht I–III." *Or* 35: 1–20; 46: 183–197.

Sokoloff, Michael. 1974. *The Targum to Job from Qumran Cave XI*. Bar-Ilan Studies in Near Eastern Languages and Culture. Ramat Gan: Bar-Ilan University.

Sokoloff, Michael. 2017. *A Dictionary of Jewish Palestinian Aramaic of the Byzantine Period*. Dictionaries of Talmud, Midrash and Targum 1 and Publications of the Comprehensive Aramaic Lexicon Project. 3rd Revised and Expanded Edition. Ramat Gan: Bar-Ilan University.

Sokoloff, Michael. 2020. *A Dictionary of Jewish Babylonian Aramaic of the Talmudic and Geonic Periods*. Dictionaries of Talmud, Midrash and Targum 3 and Publications of the Comprehensive Aramaic Lexicon Project. Ramat Gan: Bar-Ilan University.

van der Spek, Robartus. 2015. "*Madinatu* = URU^{meš} 'Satrapy, Province, District, Country' in Late Babylonian." *AfO* 53: 110–116.

Streck, Michael P. 2003. *Die akkadischen Verbalstämme mit ta-Infix*. AOAT 303. Münster: Ugarit Verlag.

Streck, Michael P. 2005. "Simply a Seller, Nothing but Gods: The Nominal Suffix *-ān* in Old Babylonian." In *Memoriae Igor M. Diakonoff*. Papers of the Institute of Oriental and Classical Studies 8. Babel und Bibel 2, edited by Leonid E. Kogan, Natalia V. Koslova, Sergey Loesov, and Sergey Tishchenko, 233–243. Winona Lake, Ind: Eisenbrauns.

Streck, Michael P. 2007. Review of CAD P. *ZA* 97: 149–152.

Streck, Michael Paul. 2010. "Feminine Gender of Old Babylonian Nouns." In *Von Göttern und Menschen. Beiträge zu Literatur und Geschichte des Alten Orients. Festschrift für Brigitte Groneberg*, CM 41, edited by Dahlia Shehata, Frauke Weiershäuser, and Kamran Vincent Zand, 287–305. Leiden: Brill.

Streck, Michael P. 2018. *Supplements to the Akkadian Dictionaries*. 1: B, P. LAOS 7, 1. Wiesbaden: Harrassowitz.

Tal, Abraham. 2000. *A Dictionary of Samaritan Aramaic* 1–2. HdO I 50. Leiden: Brill.

Waerzeggers, Caroline. 2010. *The Ezida Temple of Borsippa: Priesthood, Cult, Archives*. Achaemenid History 15. Leiden: Nederlands Instituut voor het Nabije Oosten.

Zadok, Ran. 1978. *On West Semites in Babylonia during the Chaldean and Achaemenian Periods: An Onomastic Study*. Tel Aviv: Tel Aviv University.

Zadok, Ran. 1997. "On Aromatics and Reeds." NABU 1997: 51–52 (no. 55).
Zadok, Ran. 2009. *Catalogue of Documents from Borsippa or Related to Borsippa in the British Museum* 1. NISABA 21. Messina: Dipartimento di Scienze dell'Antichità dell'Università degli Studi di Messina.
Zadok, Ran. 2020. "Arameo-Akkadica II." NABU 2020: 266–269 (no. 128).
Zadok, Ran. 2021a. "On Aramaic Loanwords in Neo- and Late-babylonian Texts: Introduction and Semantic-Topical Taxonomy (Part One)." IOS 21: 71–135.
Zadok, Ran. 2021b. "Additamenta to Arameo-Akkadica." NABU 2021: 131–137 (no. 56).
Zadok, Ran. 2021c. "Lexical Notes." *AuOr* 39: 125–127.

PART 2

Semitic Languages and Linguistics

CHAPTER 5

The Way to the Rainy Mountains: Semantic Networks of Natural Metaphors in Najdi Poetry

Letizia Cerqueglini | ORCID: 0000-0001-7615-8427
Tel Aviv University
cerqueglini@tauex.tau.ac.il

Abstract

Landscape and weather are rich experimental fields for exploring metaphoric thinking about both shared experience and language-specific construction. I analyze the distribution of metaphoric "water" subdomains (clouds/rain/stream/well/flood/mountain peak/sea) across the target domains of emotions/poetry/threat in Najdi poetry compared to other Arabian traditions, mainly Modern South Arabian. Results show that, in constructing metaphors, the cognitive experience of landscape influences cultural interpretations and linguistic expressions. In structuring metaphoric networks two forces interact: landscape specific ecological differences and cultural contact. The physical experience of different landscapes restricts the transmigration of linguistic and cultural influences in landscape based metaphoric imagery.

Keywords

Najdi Arabic – Modern South Arabian – Landscape-based Metaphors – Language, Culture and Nature

תקציר

נוף ומזג אוויר הם מרחבים ניסיוניים עשירים לחקר חשיבה מטפורית על חוויות משותפות ועל מבנים ייחודיים לשפה. אני מנתחת את התפלגות תת-התחומים המטפוריים של "מים" (עננים/גשם/נחל/באר/שיטפון/פסגת הרים/ים) על פני תחומי המטרה של רגשות/שירה/איום בשירה הנג׳דית בהשוואה למסורות אחרות בחצי האי הערב, בעיקר מסורות דרום-ערביות חדשות. התוצאות מראות כי בבניית מטפורות, החוויה הקוגניטיבית של הנוף משפיעה על פרשנויות תרבותיות וביטויים לשוניים. בבניית רשתות מטפוריות שני כוחות מקיימים אינטראקציה: הבדלים אקולוגיים ספציפיים לנוף ומגע תרבותי. החוויה הפיזית של נופים שונים מגבילה את המעבר של השפעות לשוניות ותרבותיות בדימויים מטפוריים מבוססי נוף.

 | DOI:10.1163/9789004526822_006

מילות מפתח

ערבית נג׳דית – דרום-ערבית חדשה – מטפורות מבוססות נוף – שפה, תרבות וטבע

المستخلص

المناظر الطبيعية والطقس هي مجالات تجريبية غنية لاستكشاف التفكير المجازي حول كل من الخبرة المشتركة والبناء الخاص بلغة معينة. أقوم بتحليل توزيع النطاقات الفرعية "المائية" المجازية (السحب / المطر / التيار / البئر / الفيضانات / قمة الجبل / البحر) عبر المجالات المستهدفة وهي العواطف / الشعر / التهديد في الشعر النجدي مقارنةً بالتقاليد العربية الأخرى ، وخاصةً اللغات العربية الجنوبية الحديثة. تظهر النتائج أنه في بناء الاستعارات ، تؤثر التجربة المعرفية للمناظر الطبيعية على التفسيرات الثقافية والتعبيرات اللغوية. في هيكلة الشبكات المجازية تتفاعل قوتان: الاختلافات البيئية الخاصة بالمناظر الطبيعية والاتصال الثقافي. تحد التجربة المادية للمناظر الطبيعية المختلفة من انتقال التأثيرات اللغوية والثقافية إلى الصور المجازية القائمة على المناظر الطبيعية.

الكلمات المفتاحيّة

اللغة العربية النجدية – اللغات العربية الجنوبية الحديثة – الاستعارات المبنية على المناظر الطبيعية – اللغة والثقافة والطبيعة

1 Introduction

1.1 *Landscape in Metaphors*

Landscape is one of the most influential factors in shaping cognition and language (Mark et al. 2011; Palmer et al. 2017). Like spatial and temporal categories, landscape and weather are rich experimental fields for exploring metaphoric thinking about both shared experience and language-specific construction. Embodied physical perceptions comprise the cognitive basis of metaphorical communication (Lakoff 1993), and abstract experiences are better communicated through physical phenomena (Evans and Green 2006). This research focusses on metaphors centered on the source domain of "water" in Najdi Arabic oral poetry from the Dawāsir and ʿUtaybah Bedouin confederations, based on the poetic corpus collected by Kurpershoek (1994–2002).

Metaphoric relationships between concepts represent dynamic semantic networks (Richens 1956), which have been exploited since antiquity to improve mnemonic techniques (*Porphyry On Aristotle Categories*; Strange 2014). Najdi oral poetry largely resorts to mnemonic techniques and formulaic patterns in composition and transmission, employing complex networks of recursive metaphors. Poetic language was ideal for this study, being a source of metaphor networks and a locus of their creative implementation (Herzog 2012).

The introductory sections, **Nature and Culture in the Bedouin Arab World** and **Water in Life, Language, and Cognition**, provide historical and geographical background on the ecological and literary salience of water across ancient and modern cultures of the Arabian Peninsula. The final section, **Water and its Subdomains as a Metaphor Source in Najdi Poetry**, compares Najdi and Modern South Arabian (MSA) water metaphors. Speaking different languages, expressing different literary traditions, and sharing the same environmental features only partially, Najdi and MSA societies employ different metaphor networks with some similarities due to cultural contact. This study contributes to the current research on the relationship between language and landscape (Nie and Chen 2008; Watson and Al-Mahri 2017).

1.2 *Nature and Culture in the Bedouin Arab World*

The salience of natural forces is prominent among the Bedouin tribes that originally inhabited the Arabian Peninsula and later spread into Asia and Africa. In Arabia, the prayers for rain are central in the Safaitic corpus:

> *h bʿls*$_1$*mn rwḥ b-mṭr*
>
> O Bʿls$_1$mn, send the winds with rain!
>
> AL-JALLAD 2015, 146

The Quran emphasizes that the one true God, not the pre-Islamic gods, grants different varieties of rain (*maṭar, ġayṯ, wadq, wabil, ġadaq, tall, rajʿ*) (Ali-Zargar 2014: 112). In traditional Bedouin formulaic language, poetry, narrative, and daily speech, expressions related to weather phenomena which are pervasively used to preserve the knowledge necessary for survival in the desert.

Drought is perceived as a cause of perturbation of the individual and social balance:

> *al-maḥal yisūgak ʿāl- ʿadūwak*
>
> Drought will drive you even toward your foe.
>
> BAILEY 2004, 29

Landscape elements and weather phenomena are the main sources of metaphorical transfer of emotions (Al-Ghadeer 2009; Ḥusayn 1926; Ritt-Benmimoun 2009; Slyomovics 2020; Socin 1900):

walʿēn yā fahad daffigat māh ṣaḥḥābitin ṣalf al-ḥabāyib ṭiḥūdah

Oh Fahad my eyes have shed their tears, like a cloud battered by winds (from north and south).

SEELEY 2015, 86–87

fi l-barr čanni fi midīǧ al-lahābīb lēn ixtalaft w-habb fi-l-galb tansīm

In the open desert I felt as if hemmed in by walls, while the winds of moodiness tugged at my heart.

KURPERSHOEK 1994, 138–139

khatarha sirib ʿazīz kēf nasha nsill bih

Memories stirred of the beloved should I release, I'm flooded by them.

ABU-LUGHOD 1986a

Bedouin cultures preserve a sidereal season calendar anchored in the cycles of relevant celestial bodies, especially stars (Steele 2007):

al-burbārah limma tṣīr li-suhayl rišī, ʿišī wala hū ʿišī,
awwal ar-rabīaʿ w-āxir aš-štī

When Sirius hangs over Canopus like a pail rope, nightfall or just before, it's the beginning of spring and winter's end.

BAILEY 2004, 22

wagt aṯ-ṯurayya, wagt ar-rimāya

The time of the Pleiades is the time for sowing.

BAILEY 2004, 71

The association of sidereal bodies, cardinal directions, and weather phenomena is used to construct symbols and metaphors that refer to collective ethical and esthetic values and personal feelings. The star Canopus, low in the southern horizon for a short period, brings violent floods and is ominously associated with betrayal, inconstancy, and guilt:

ʿugb aš-šaḥam ğid hi ğidīd al-manāšīf mann aḏ-ḏma misyāfha yōm zāni
čanha hašīm aṭ-ṭalḥ tamši gifāgīf ḥazzat miġīb shēl w-il-gēḏ dāni

Once covered with fat, they now look like shriveled thongs: cruel thirst robbed them of the strength they gained from spring's pastures. Like a bundle of dead acacia wood they trudge along at the time of Canopus' eclipse when the great heat sets in.

KURPERSHOEK 1994, 160

in tiliʿ suhayl lā tāmin as-sayl lō kān ʿagāb al-layl

If Canopus has appeared beware of a flood, even toward the end of the night.

BAILEY 2004, 31

In contrast, Polaris, fixed and constant, represents the positive character of the northern direction:

ġāb an-niğm was-suhayl, wal-ğidī mā ġāb

The Pleiades disappear as Canopus too, but Polaris never sinks in the sky.

BAILEY 1974, 583

In traditional Bedouin societies, naturalistic metaphors play an important role in the communicative code, representing the speaker's adhesion to the common and communicable experiential heritage (Abu-Lughod 1986b; Al-Rassi 1987). Nature is a pervasive source of images used to communicate messages that cannot or should not be referred to directly (Gibbs and Beitel 1995):

My fortune is like a flower thrown among thorns on a windy day.

AL-KRENAWI 2000

1.3 *Water in Life, Language, and Cognition*

Water is an inexhaustible source of metaphors across languages and cultures (Ashliman 2005). It has tremendous influence on the imaginary thinking of Bedouin societies in arid ecosystems. In the Bedouin oral literatures, the divine power is frequently invoked and blessed for its ability or will to create life through rain and other atmospheric phenomena related to the water cycle:

yallah (…) yā xalḏin baddaw ʿišbin u-ġidrān u-fyḏin miṯl azzuwāli ḥamārah min mizintin baṭrāfha tigil ḏayyān

> Oh God (…) creator of grass and rain pools in the desert and hollows in which flowers shine red like carpets from rain clouds which seem lit up at their edges.
>
> SEELEY 2015, 72–73

illi yiʿaywiḏ mimḥlāt ad-dīrah
b-wasmi w-ṣēf w-miǧtifīh čnāni

He Who compensates drought-stricken areas
With rains of winter and late spring, and after that those of early summer.

KURPERSHOEK 1995, 226–227

As in *nabaṭī* poetry (Holes 2011), rain is described in the Najd according to different characteristics and the season to which it pertains (Robertson 1932). In the Sinai and Negev (and in Classical Arabic), *wasm* designates spring rains (Bailey 1994, 71), and *šitiy*, autumn/winter rains. In the Najd, *wasm* indicates the autumn/winter rains (Kurpershoek 1999, 480), while *rabiʿ*, the pan-Arabic term for "spring," also designates spring rains (Kurpershoek 1999, 375), just as *ṣēf*, "summer," indicates summer rains. The Najdi word *mahāwi* indicates late summer rains (Kurpershoek 1995, 460). The specific terminology for atmospheric phenomena provides temporal references for the facts described.

2 Corpus Screening

The present investigation is based on an examination of Kurpershoek's collection of Najdi poetry, published between 1993 and 2002, and referred to here as 'the corpus.' I have isolated recursive "water" metaphors in the corpus, using Carston's model (Carston 2010), which is based on relevance theory (Wilson and Sperber 2004), according to which metaphors are selected on the basis of optimal communicative immediacy and effectiveness. For example, the metaphor of the poet's ascent to the mountain and prayer for rain is a recurring motif, which is laden with real and figurative meanings related to water. The elements of this sequence are clustered in fixed patterns in the poetry of ad-Dindān. First, the poet isolates himself, driven by distress, climbing a mountain peak (which may be seen as the equivalent of the classical *nasīb* incipit; Wagner 1988). His distress may be due to offenses, slander (Kurpershoek 1994, 184–185), nostalgia for places and people, or drought. Having reached the lonely peak, described as an outpost or a nest of dark-winged ravens (Kurpershoek

1994, 106–107), he bursts into poetic verses and, often, tears. He addresses his own heart and God, asking for rain. The prayer continues with a review of all the places that should be blessed and restored by the water (Kurpershoek 1999, 142–143), and culminates in the appearance of camel herds in the regenerated landscapes. Descriptions and praises of these animals and/or of tribal knights (Kurpershoek 1994, 106–107) represent the last section of this type of composition, considered a poetic genre *per se* in ad-Dindān's production, defined as "the rain prayers" (ibid., 62–64).

Each element of this formulaic cluster is linked to the others by a dense network of subtle references. The poetic fulguration is manifested in flashes and clouds surrounding distant nocturnal horizons, animals' coats reflect the sudden lightning's bright glow, and both landscapes and animals awaken comforting memories and images (Kurpershoek 1994, 172–173, verse 13):

yarfuḏ ribābih fi trābih mičāhīb,
čannih miǧāhīr al-ǧahām al-miǧāhīm

Slanting curtains of rain pouring down on the earth,
as if they were the calves of herds of black camels.

KURPERSHOEK 1994, 140–141

lēn ixtalaft w-habb fi l-galb tansīm,
ašūf fi ṣadri čima sāyiḥ as-sīb,
yašrab ʿala māh al-ǧahām ar-ruwādīm

While the winds of moodiness tugged at my heart.
You'd say inside my heart a little stream welled forth,
its water gulped down by large, mixed herds of camels.

KURPERSHOEK 1994, 138–139

In ad-Dindān, the poet claims his beneficial role in society in the request for rain, while in other poetry, the prayer on the mountain top may include personal benefits (Kurpershoek 1999, 164–165):

ʿaddēt rās Mḥaywwah bēn Abānēn
al-haḏbh illi ʿind xašm az-zibārah
ya-llah ṭalabtik min ḥalāl al-bixīlīn

I climbed to the top of Mḥayyiwah between the Abānāt,
An isolated rock standing at the edge of the dunes,
Praying, "O God, bestow on me the livestock of the misers."
ŠLĒWĪḤ IBN MĀʿIZ AL-ʿAṬĀWI; KURPERSHOEK 1995, 198–199

While ad-Dindān uses the formulaic scene sequence as a fixed pattern, other poets use these scenes as formulaic elements that link different sequences within variously themed lyrics. Nevertheless, water metaphors, especially as opposed to aridity and drought metaphors, are semantically consistent among all authors in the corpus.

The examination of the corpus revealed that the source domain "water" is articulated into subdomains: "clouds," "well," "stream," "rainstorm," "rain," and, rarely, "sea," mainly used for three target domains: emotions, poetry, and threat. Furthermore, "water," as "rain" and "clouds," is present in greetings, blessings, and poetic compositions not as metaphors but as explicit similitudes, as in *zamil* (Caton 1991), the traditional northern Yemenite poetic genre, and more generally in all *nabaṭī* poetry (Holes 2011). The term *nabaṭī* designates all Najdi vernacular poetry, including Kurpershoek's collection, i.e., the corpus:

sallim ʿalēhum ʿidd ma nša min al-waddān

Bring them greetings numerous as clouds amassing on the horizon.
KURPERSHOEK 1994, 182–183

sallim ʿalēh ʿdād wablin miṭarha

Salute him as many times as drops of rain fall from the sky.
KURPERSHOEK 2002, 440–441

ʿasa dārhum ʿugb ar-ribīʿ tṣāf

May their homeland be blessed with rains in spring and summer.
KURPERSHOEK 2002, 516–517

In contrast, curses are expressed by wishing drought:

midhālhum la sigāh al-wabil marrētih mitšāliyin lēn ǧītih wi-l-bala ǧāni

May the clouds pass over their tribal haunts without releasing their rain.
KURPERSHOEK 1994, 188–189

3 Water and It Subdomains as a Metaphor Source in Najdi Poetry

In Najdi poetry, each stage of the water cycle is embodied in positive and negative images, with positive connotations by far more numerous than negative ones. This is probably due to the Najd's aridity, an all too real threat to survival.

3.1 *Emotions*

The target domain of emotions is represented by the subdomains of clouds, wells, and the sea. Distress is often described in terms of fire, thirst, and dryness of land, heart, and mind, or a drained well whose bottom is scraped and from which the water of tears gushes:

tahayyaḏ w-wann w-ḏamrih čann fīh išʿāl,
w-čann aš-šbūb mwallaʿin fīh tōlīʿi

Grief welled up and he moaned as if roasted,
by a fire that had been lit in his breast.
KURPERSHOEK 1994, 114–115

Some passages refer to dryness as emotional pain (Kurpershoek 1994, 150–151; Kurpershoek 1999, 246–247). In ad-Dindān's compositions, once the poet is on the peak and emotions mount as the clouds thicken, he calls upon his own heart, dried up by sadness (Kurpershoek 1994, 160–161):

fāḥ damʿ al-ʿēn la ṭarraw al-ʿaṣir al-gidīm,
fōḥ figrin bīḥ saddih wu-hu bīrih riğiʿ,
al-mğāmiʿ wi-l-mfārig ğaʿal galbi hašīm,
hašim zarb al-bān fōg aṣ-ṣifa ğid hu xalīʿ

When I hear mention of the days of yore tears well up,
Like water in an abandoned well that is dug up again,
The many meetings and partings rent my heart,
Like withered twigs of *bān*-trees that fell down onto the boulders.
KURPERSHOEK 1994, 114–115

Another example is "My heart's pent-up anxieties burst forth in sobs and sighs, like thirsty herds rushing to the well" (Kurpershoek 1999, 140–141). Dry winds blowing on the heart and destroying its crop metaphorically represent uneasiness (Kurpershoek 1994, 138–139). Rain is the balm that extinguishes the heat of feelings and the prayer for rain is also the prayer for a remedy for emotional discomfort. On rare occasions, the sea, unfamiliar to southern Najdi poets, is evoked in its fury to represent the disruptive force of strong and uncontrolled emotions:

al-baḥr la fāḏ ma šayyin yiḏāmih
ṭamm ḥatta l-naww min fōg az-zuwāmi

When the sea surges, nothing has the power to contain it:
Even the clouds above the hilltops are swept up by its waters
KURPERSHOEK 1994, 176–177

3.2 *Poetry*

The subdomain of "rain" is not an explicit metaphor for poetry, but rather a polysemous symbol of both divine and poetic creativity. Rain represents relief from drought, as poetry and tears are comfort for sadness. The metaphor that links "water" to both verses and tears is frequently made explicit by figurative extensions in which the poet sees his tears as a stream which floods the valley:

aġanni b-gāfin lēn ǧa lli warāh nhāl,
w-ṣakkat ʿalayy ǧill al-ǧuwāriʿ mahānīʿi,
ana damʿ ʿēni ḥasbi allah ʿala l-anḏāl,
ġawārīb sēlih ḏayyigann al-mahāyīʿi

No sooner did I chant one verse,
than others came like camels rushing to a well,
Pressing around me and lowering their big heads to the water.
My tears flowed—may God protect me against the wretches—
Until its copious stream filled every confluence of the valley.
KURPERSHOEK 1994, 116–117

Tears and poetry are both associated with water streaming, in the positive, fertilizing sense. The poet's effort to express confused, violent feelings in verse resembles a sacrifice that re-establishes a primeval cosmic order, similar to the regular alternation between rainy and dry seasons:

ṭālibk lēlin min al-mašrig lya l-ḥarrah,
bargih ʿagūgin ḥagūgin fīh rannāni

> From you I ask a night stretching from the east towards al-Ḥarrah,
> heralded by flashes of lightning and rolling thunder
> as unmistakable signs.
>
> KURPERSHOEK 1994, 106–107

The actual metaphoric subdomain for "poetry" is the streaming water.

The mountain peak, where clouds gather to release rain (Caton 1991), becomes a metaphorical subdomain of "water" for poetic inspiration, i.e., the place where passions find an outlet. This catharsis restores order, contemplated from on high: "I climbed the peak of a lofty mountain against my wish, driven to that high vantage point by the poetic urge" (Kurpershoek 1994, 144–145).

3.3 *Threat*

Water turns from blessing into catastrophe when rainstorms devastate inhabited lands, sweeping away men and animals and washing away the fields:

> *inna čima nawwin sibag bārǧih māh*
> *min ṭāḥ fi diglātna ma šaḥanna*
>
> We are like a rainstorm that is announced by lightning,
> indifferent to the fate of those who are swept up by us.
>
> KURPERSHOEK 2002, 220–221

In particular, water's injurious power is expressed in the description of conflicts: clouds and thunder mean threats, as they are followed by "rains of bullets," while the troops invade the field as a flood:

> *ʿala Ṭalāl aṣ-ṣibḥ xilt maxāyil*
> *tāṣal maxāyilḥa lya l-Ğirḏāwi*
> *brūgha l-hindi w-sallāt al-ʿağam*
> *wi-ṯʿūlha l-ğinyān wa-l-ʿazāwi*
> *timṭir bi-ʿaṭšān al-mḥabbab wa-l-ğana*
> *miṯl al-ğarād maʿ al-ḥamād ad-dāwi*
> *ğāna Sʿūd msayyirin bi-ğmūʿih*
>
> In the morning I saw thunderclouds over Ṭalāl,
> A compact mass extending as far as al-Jirḏāwi,
> Its lightning: Indian steel and Persian blades,
> Its showers: javelins and tribal battle cries,
> Spraying fiery bullets and rains of spears,

Thick as swarms of locusts floating over the barren plains.
It was Sʿūd, marching his armed bands on us.
KURPERSHOEK 1995, 180–181

tanahhaḏ at min ğarr Ṣabḥa maxīlah
b-sēlin yiṭimm al-ʿirğ wi-l-ʿadām
ṣabbat w-anṣibat w-inṣabb māha w-ṣabṣibat
bi-mšawwakin yašḏi silīb iʿḏām

From Ṣabḥa's watercourse a dark mass of clouds arose,
unleashing a torrent that flooded the dunes and undulating sands,
pouring down its waters relentlessly and persistently,
in a hail of bullets that splice and shatter the enemy's bones.
KURPERSHOEK 2002, 674–677

Clouds, with thunder and lightning, are usually positive signs of rain:

ya-llah b-lēlin ma yixuffih nisam l-anwād

God give us a night whose clouds are not dispersed by the winds.
KURPERSHOEK 1994, 39

Yet clouds also represent ominous signs of threat, metaphors of upcoming battles:

nawwin ḥadar gāmat tigaṣṣaf rʿudih
amṭar ʿala Yāmin b-suww al-ʿaḏābi

A large cloud came down from the sky with loud thunderclaps
releasing a deluge that brought death and destruction to Yām.
KURPERSHOEK 2002, 656–657

The threatening character of floods, often unexpected, is associated with both the physical and emotional spheres of human experience. In the following passage, the poet is overwhelmed by an irresistible inspiration and seems to burst into a devastating torrent of verses with a complex metaphorical texture:

miṯl sēlin ḥadar min rūs šiʿbāni
la ğa ʿḏātin b-wasṭ aš-šiʿb yazwīha

Like a torrent rushing down from the higher valleys,
sweeping up any tree that happens to stand in its course.

KURPERSHOEK 2002, 652–653

4 Biodiversity and Cultural Contact

Water seems to be a universal source of metaphors for life and psychic intensity, as opposed to physical and emotional drought (e.g., Italian *uomo arido,* lit. "arid man," i.e., man without feelings). Nonetheless, the structure and extension of metaphorical networks centered on water are shaped by both landscape-based and culture-specific constraints. Even geographically contiguous and culturally connected societies may select different natural elements as metaphor sources and map different meanings onto them (Orlove 2003). "Water" subdomains are used as metaphor sources in both Najdi and Modern South Arabian poetry, with evident similarities. In the poetic imagery of the Mahra *fasīh* (Liebhaber 2010), the poet's ascent to the mountain peak where clouds thicken before rain is well represented (Gasparini and Al-Mahri, forthcoming). The metaphor of drought as absence of poetry is made explicit here:

śmīmet enṭərōr teh bālī ksē
yšeṭṭem ḥarḳ we-ryīḥ we-lhēb
w-xeyr yemyōl law menh eysēr
wet nhā beh tetrūb be-bhēl

Would that God might give us rain in the canyon of Śmīmet Neṭrōr
It has struggled against the drought, the wind and fire for long enough.
Let goodness return, certainly it's much better.
While we are there, words turned to dust.

LIEBHABER 2018, *The Dog Days of Summer*

The prayer for rain (*fi'óse lə-méṡɛ*) is also found in Soqotra (Naumkin and Kogan 2015, 334–339), Rain, invoked as the benevolent aspect of the divine, favors nature and animals and drives away evil. Mahra poets more often associate dry winds with painful emotions, while the humid southern winds from the sea, rather than rains, are invoked for relief:

ṯʿār ḳāten w-ṭarbūt hel mǧawrī ḏ-rīḥeyn wet ġmūzem w-klūb
we-ṭwōren emdīt beyn edōṯer we-rbē feyṣel ḥawlī ḳlūb
ṣrōme mehhəbīb ṯʿār elēhen mātlīm ān ewakb ertəkūb

Atop the peak of Ṭarbūt at the place of the paths of the winds when they blow furiously and are joined together.
Sometimes (there comes) the sea breeze between the stars of Dōṯer and Rbē (when) the first season has come [or finished, lit. "happened"].
Now I'll compose a *habbōt* atop a well-crafted melody if the rhymes fit together.

LIEBHABER 2018, *Atop the Peak of Ṭarbūt*

l-ād ār emdīt hēkā w-zefzīf
mezrūt b-ğawf w-źeyḳī erīf

Only the cold, southwest wind remains blowing back and forth
It blows into my chest and makes the countryside constricting.

LIEBHABER 2018, *Homesick in Najrn*

ğwāher hōnet we-mdīt w-līn tḳaźfen elhēb

Ğwāher is a fragrant breeze and the south wind that extinguishes our burning.

LIEBHABER 2018, *Advice for Ğwāher*

In both Najdi and MSA poetry, "water" subdomains have positive and negative values. Yet in the MSA tradition, negative meanings (violence/threat/fatality) appear frequently (seven of the twelve metaphors in Liebhaber's works mentioned here), while they are rare in the Najdi corpus (sixteen of 127 water-based metaphors). Mahra poets associate clouds with military threats and streaming water with devastating fatalities (Liebhaber 2013) more often than with positive phenomena:

fōn eġawreb ezernīw bāl ezōyed ḏe-ġbēr zehmōten le-ġrūb
eḏhībeh yeṭmūm le-ğdēd ebelyōt we-k-ṣamt yekbūb
we-ġźāb eźeymet ḳā we-ġyīm l-ḥārwāḥ w-helmen eṭma ksūb

I've known from before the thundering rain clouds the one that brings great quantities of dust sheets of rain from water-buckets,
Its flood covers the earth even up to the ancient highlands with violence (the flood) rolls down,
Its roiling surge encompasses the land sending clouds over all of humankind and snatches away everything that is valuable.

LIEBHABER 2018, *Atop the Peak of Ṭarbūt*

wāt śōret nwūt men śī men nkīf
eźhūr ḳeywōy we-yšāzīf (...)
ḏ-ār kād xdōm ezey lekfīf
men bād emwēǧ w-ḳeźź we-ldīf
tlōbed śwōr we-shīb yexfīf

When the rain storms arise and anything is in the way of the stationary clouds
The backs [of the people] are strong and are steadfast [against them]
All those who work should protect his flock
After the waves and [their] roaring and crashing
[Until] it becomes calm again and the waves diminish.

LIEBHABER 2018, *Homesick in Najrn*

neǧm ertəbūb w-hen men ḥōmer ḏ-ḥeklī nēweh ʿādeh ān ṭbūt
ḥemlet arḳās men eremš ḏe-kṣē yexlīlen ebyūt
ār xlūṭem šeh nǧūm men ʿāṣef ḏe-ryiḥ we-tḳawleb ḏ-bīlōt

The rain-star about to burst and thunder at the edge of the eastern clouds the downpour is about to come.
They fall upon Arḳās from mouths of the black thunderheads they come through the roofs of the houses.
Other rain-stars have arrived with them on the storms of winds that become like those of desert.

LIEBHABER 2018, *Gunfight in Niśṭawn*

As in Najdi poetry, in the Classical Arabic *qaṣīda*, the association of floods with battling troops is infrequent (Stetkevych 1993). In the Najdi corpus, sudden, devastating raids are more often represented by metaphors of swarms of locusts and clouds of dust (35 times) than by floods (16 times). The water cycle is of such crucial importance in the Najd that its mention in negative contexts may be considered ominous.

Finally, the sea is in wide use in the Mahra and Śḥéri poetic traditions, while it appears rarely in the Najdi metaphoric landscapes (three occurrences in Kurpershoek's corpus), often as a threat:

ʿār xźeyr w-lō ʿāmūm we-shīb ḏ-īḳḳədūt le-mkawser we-nkəśūt

Like the ocean when it is angry waves follow upon waves over the reefs [the ocean] roils.

LIEBHABER 2018, *The Battle of ʾĀḳəbbōt*

Ya rábbi ilkún ḥanófi be-ḏ̣aíq
Be-raúrem xḏ̣aír, wu-sé tġaléq

Lord, may my soul not be in troubles,
In the green sea, when it closes the way out.
MÜLLER 1907, 155

5 Conclusions

I have analyzed the distribution of metaphoric "water" subdomains (clouds/rain/stream/well/flood/mountain peak/sea) across the target domains of emotions, poetry, and threat in Najdi poetry. Other Arabian traditions were considered for comparison.

In constructing metaphors, the cognitive experience of landscape influences cultural interpretations and linguistic expressions. In the Najdi and MSA traditions, the mountain peak is seen as a subdomain of "water" and is an integral part of its metaphorical network, as it is cognitively connected to the formation of clouds. Cardinal directions associated with weather phenomena are also part of the "water" network. The southern wind, a metaphor for drought in the Najd, in MSA poetry represents the humid sea breeze.

The trajectories of extension and boundaries of the metaphoric "water" network in the Najdi corpus are ruled by the "partiality of metaphor" principle, according to which in a conceptual metaphor not all correspondences between source and target domain must be applied or activated (Lakoff and Johnson 1999, 53–54). That is, cognitive networks that link physical experiences are only partly exploited in metaphorical transfer, according to cognitive and/or cultural specificities (e.g., English "cold/chilly/ice" represent lack of emotions, unlike "snow/floe/snowball"). Thus, not all physical manifestations of water (i.e., the subdomains of the source) express all metaphoric (or target) domains.

In MSA poetry, "water" subdomains are used more frequently as images of threat than they are in the Najdi corpus, probably because in the coastal MSA homelands, drought is a less constant threat and rainfall is heavier and more regular. Winds, characterized by the cardinal direction of their provenance, and the sea are pervasively used as sources of metaphorical transfer.

These results confirm the existence of landscape-specific differences in structuring metaphoric networks, alongside the impressive results of cultural contact as observed by Liebhaber (2015)—between the MSA and *nabaṭī* poetic traditions. In sum, the experience of different landscapes restricts the transmigration of linguistic and cultural influences in landscape-based metaphoric imagery.

References

Abu-Lughod, Lila. 1986a. *Veiled Sentiments*. Berkeley: University of California.

Abu-Lughod, Lila. 1986b. "Modest Women, Subversive Poems: The Politics of Love in an Egyptian Bedouin Society." *Bulletin of British Society for Middle Eastern Studies* 13: 159–168.

Al-Ghadeer, Moneera. 2009. *Desert Voices. Bedouin Women's Poetry in Saudi Arabia.* London: Bloomsbury.

Ali Zargar, Cyrus. 2014. "Water." In *Islamic Images and Ideas: Essays on Sacred Symbolism*, edited by John Andrew Morrow, 112–123. Jefferson, NC: McFarland.

Al-Jallad, Ahmad. 2015. *An Outline of the Grammar of the Safaitic Inscriptions*. Leiden: Brill.

Al-Krenawi, Alean. 2000. "Bedouin-Arab Clients' Use of Proverbs in the Therapeutic Setting." *International Journal for the Advancement of Counselling* 22: 91–102.

Al-Rassi, Salim. 1987. *Folklore, Stories, Proverbs and Wise Sayings*. (Arabic). Beirut: Moassaat Nofal.

Ashliman, Dee. 2005. "Water spirits". In *Archetypes and Motifs in Folklore and Literature: A Handbook*, edited by Jane Garry and Hasan El-Shamy, 210–216. Armonk—New York—London: M.E. Sharpe.

Bailey, Clinton. 1974. "Bedouin Star-Lore in Sinai and the Negev." *Bulletin of the School of Oriental and African Studies* 37: 580–590

Bailey, Clinton. 2004. *A Culture of Desert Survival: Bedouin Proverbs from Sinai and the Negev*. New Haven: Yale University.

Carston, Robyn. 2010. "Metaphor: Ad hoc Concepts, Literal Meaning and Mental Images." *Proceedings of the Aristotelian Society* 110: 295–321.

Caton, Steven. 1991. *"Peaks of Yemen I Summon": Poetry as Cultural Practice in a North Yemeni Tribe*. Berkeley: University of California.

Evans, Vyvyan and Melanie Green. 2006. *Cognitive Linguistics: An Introduction*. Edinburgh: Edinburgh University.

Gasparini, Fabio and Saeed Al-Mahri. forthcoming. "Water and Culture among the MSAL-Speaking People of Dhofar". In *Language and Nature in Southern and Eastern Arabia.*

Gibbs, Raymond and Dinara Beitel. 1995. "What Proverb Understanding Reveals about How People Think." *Psychological Bulletin* 118: 133–154.

Herzog, Thomas. 2012. "Orality and the Tradition of Arabic Epic Storytelling". In *Medieval Oral Literature*, edited by Karl Reichl, 627–645. Berlin: de Gruyter.

Holes Clive. 2011. "Nabaṭī Poetry, Language of." In *Encyclopedia of Arabic Language and Linguistics*, Managing Editors Online Edition, Lutz Edzard and Rudolf de Jong. Consulted online on 20 March 2022. http://dx.doi.org/10.1163/1570-6699_eall_EALL_sim_000031

Ḥusayn, Taha. 1926. *Fi-š-šiʿr al-ǧāhilī*. Cairo: Dār al-Kutub.

Kurpershoek, Marcel. 1994–2002. *Oral Poetry and Narratives from Central Arabia*. Vols. 1–4. Leiden: Brill.

Lakoff, George. 1993. "The Contemporary Theory of Metaphor." In *Metaphor and Thought*, edited by Andrew Ortony, 202–252. Cambridge: Cambridge University.

Lakoff, George and Mark Johnson. 1999. *Philosophy in the Flesh: The Embodied Mind and Its Challenge to Western Thought*. New York: Basic Books.

Liebhaber, Samuel. 2010. "Written Mahri, Mahri Fuṣḥā and Their Implications for Early Historical Arabic." *Proceedings of the Seminar for Arabian Studies* 40: 227–232.

Liebhaber, Samuel. 2013. "Rhetoric, Rite-of-Passage and the Multilingual Poetics of Arabia." *Journal of Middle Eastern Literatures* 16: 118–146.

Liebhaber, Samuel. 2015. "Mahri Oral Poetry and Arabic Nabaṭī Poetry: Common Core, Divergent Outcomes." *Arabian Humanities* 5. doi.org/10.4000/cy.2973

Liebhaber, Samuel. 2018. *When Melodies Gather: The Oral Art of the Mahra*. Stanford: Stanford University. http://whenmelodiesgather.supdigital.org/wmg/

Mark, David, Andrew Turk, Niclas Burenhult and David Stea. 2011. *Landscape in Language*. Amsterdam: John Benjamins.

Müller, Heinrich.1907. *Südarabische Expedition*, Band VII. Vienna: Alfred Hölder.

Nie, Yaning and Rong Chen. 2008. "WATER Metaphors and Metonymies in Chinese: A Semantic Network." *Pragmatics & Cognition* 16: 492–516.

Orlove, Benjamin. 2003. "How People Name Seasons." In *Weather, Climate, Culture*, edited by Sarah Strauss and Benjamin Orlove, 121–137. London: Berg.

Palmer, Bill, Jonathon Lum, Jonathan Schlossberg and Alice Gaby. 2017. "How Does the Environment Shape Spatial Language? Evidence for Sociotopography." *Linguistic Typology* 21: 457–491.

Richens, Richard. 1956. "General Program for Mechanical Translation between Any Two Languages via an Algebraic Interlingua." *Report on Research: Cambridge Language Research Unit* 3: 37

Ritt-Benmimoun, Veronika. 2009. "Bedouin Women's Poetry in Southern Tunisia." *Estudios de dialectología Norteafricana y Andalusí* 13: 217–233.

Robertson, Edward. 1932. "Rain, Dew, Snow, and Cloud in Arab Proverb." *Journal of the American Oriental Society* 52: 145–158.

Sergeant, Robert 1951. *Prose and Poetry from Hadramawt. South Arabian Poetry I*. London: Taylor's Foreign Press.

Seeley, Maira. 2015. "Real Bedouin Words: Orality, Moral Authority, and Bedouin Women's Poetry in Contemporary Jordan." *Nomadic Peoples* 19: 73–94.

Slyomovics, Susan. 2020. "The Arab Oral Epic of the Bani Hilal Tribe: Al-Sīrah al-Hilāliyyah." *The Companion to World Literature*, edited by Ken Seigneurie. Hoboken, NJ: Wiley Blackwell. doi.org/10.1002/9781118635193.ctwl0138

Socin, Albert. 1900. *Diwan aus Centralarabien*. Hildesheim: George Holms.

Sowayan, Saad. 1985. *Nabati Poetry*. Berkeley: University of California.

Steele, John. 2007. *Calendars and Years: Astronomy and Time in the Ancient Near East*. Oxford: Oxbow.

Stetkevych, Suzanne. 1993. *The Mute Immortals Speak: Pre-Islamic Poetry and the Poetics of Ritual*. Ithaca: Cornell University.

Strange, Steven. 2014. *Porphyry: On Aristotle Categories*. London: Bloomsbury.

Wagner, Ewald. 1988. *Grundzüge der klassischen arabischen Dichtung*. 2 vols. Darmstadt: Wissenschaftliche Buchgesellschaft.

Watson, Janet and Abdullah Al-Mahri. 2017. "Language and Nature in Dhofar." *"QuadRi": Quaderni di RiCOGNOZINIO* 7: 87–103.

Wilson, Deirdre and Dan Sperber. 2004. "Relevance Theory." In *The Handbook of Pragmatics*, edited by Laurence Horn and Gregory Ward, 607–632. Oxford: Blackwell.

CHAPTER 6

The Vocalization of Guttural Consonants in the *Secunda* and Other Hebrew Traditions

Isabella Maurizio | ORCID: 0000-0002-5683-9062
University "Alma Mater Studiorum", Bologna | EPHE, Paris
isabellamaurizio89@gmail.com

Abstract

The guttural consonants exhibit an influence on the vocalism in all traditions of the Hebrew language, including the autonomous tradition of the *Secunda*. However, there are some morphological forms where the *Secunda* does not present a lowering of paradigmatic vowels to /a/: These are the *yiqtol* pattern of the *qal* imperfect for verbs with first or second guttural radical consonant and the *qal* imperative for a ע״חע verb. In verbs with a guttural radical, the other Hebrew traditions, mainly the Tiberian tradition, generally have the low vowel /a/. Therefore, concerning vowel assimilation to gutturals, the different Hebrew traditions indicate unstable attitudes, oscillating between the phonetic assimilation of vowels toward /a/ by effect of guttural consonants, on one hand, and the normalization imposed by the *Systemzwang* exerted by the strong pattern, on the other hand. The *Secunda* shows the preservation of the *yiqtol* vocalic pattern and its extension to guttural verbs. Interestingly, the *Secunda* does not generally exhibit the assimilation of vowels to gutturals in the imperfect *qal* of guttural verbs, while in other forms this tendency is frequently attested.

Keywords

Guttural consonants – guttural verbs – low vowel – *Secunda* – *yiqtol* pattern

תקציר

העיצורים הגרוניים מפגינים השפעה על הווקאליזם בכל מסורות השפה העברית, כולל המסורת העצמאית של ה-'סקונדה'. עם זאת, יש כמה צורות מורפולוגיות שבהן הסקונדה אינה מציגה הנמכה של התנועות הפרדיגמטיות ל-/a/. אלו הן צורת ה-yiqtol של בנין קל עבור פעלים עם עיצור שורשי ראשון או שני גרוני ושל ציווי בניין קל עבור פועל אחד ע״חע. בפעלים בעלי עיצור שורשי גרוני,

 | DOI:10.1163/9789004526822_007

בשאר המסורות העבריות, בעיקר במסורת הטברנית, מופיעה בדרך כלל התנועה הנמוכה /a/. לכן, לגבי הידמות תנועות לעיצורים גרוניים, המסורות העבריות השונות מצביעות על עמדות לא יציבות, המתנדנדות בין הידמות פונטית של תנועות לקראת /a/ בגלל השפעת עיצורים גרוניים, מצד אחד, לבין הנורמליזציה שנכפתה על ידי ה-*Systemzwang* שהפעלים השלמים מפעילים, מצד שני. הסקונדה מציגה את שימור התבנית התנועתית של ה-yiqtol והתפשטותה לפעלים גרוניים. מעניין לציין שהסקונדה אינה מציגה בדרך כלל הידמות של תנועות לעיצורים גרוניים בצורות העתיד של בניין קל של פעלים גרוניים, בעוד שבצורות אחרות נטייה זו מתועדת לעתים קרובות.

מילות מפתח

עיצורים גרוניים – פעלים גרוניים – תנועות נמוכות – סקונדה – משקל yiqtol

المستخلص

تظهر الحروف الحلقيّة تأثيرًا على الحروف الصّوتيّة في جميع تقاليد اللّغة العبريّة، بما في ذلك التّقليد المستقلّ لـ Secunda. ومع ذلك، هناك بعض الصّيغ الصّرفيّة حيث لا يقدّم Secunda خفضًا للحروف الصّوتيّة النّموذجيّة إلى /a/. هذه هي صيغ في الوزن yiqtol من النّمط qal للأفعال ذات الحرف الحلقيّ الجذريّ الأوّل أو الثّاني وصيغة الأمر من النّمط qal من فعل واحد ע״חע. في الأفعال ذات الجذور الحلقيّة، فإنّ التّقاليد العبريّة الأخرى، وخاصّة الطّبريّة، تظهر بشكل عامّ الحرف الصوتيّ المنخفض /a/. لذلك، فيما يتعلّق بمماثلة الحروف الصّوتيّة للحروف الحلقيّة، تشير التّقاليد العبريّة المختلفة إلى مواقف غير مستقرّة، تتأرجح بين التّحوّل الصّوتيّ للأحرف الصّوتيّة تجاه / a / بتأثير الحروف الحلقيّة، من ناحية، والتّطبيع الّذي يفرضه Systemzwang الّذي يمارسه الفعل الصّحيح السّالم، من ناحية أخرى. يُظهر Secunda الحفاظ على نمط yiqtol الصّوتيّ وامتداده إلى الأفعال الحلقيّة. ومن المثير للاهتمام، أنّ Secunda لا يُظهر عادةً مماثلة الحروف الصّوتيّة للحروف الحلقيّة في qal المضارع من الأفعال الحلقيّة، بينما في صيغ أخرى، يتم إثبات هذا الاتّجاه بشكل متكرّر.

الكلمات المفتاحيّة

الحروف الحلقيّة – الأفعال الحلقيّة – حروف صوتيّة منخفضة – Secunda – الوزن yiqtol

1 Introduction

The reading tradition of Biblical Hebrew was fixed from seventh to tenth century C.E. by the Masoretic punctuation (Dotan 1981), which inserted into the text not only the signs of vowels but also the *ṭeʿamim*. Both vowels and *ṭeʿamim* aimed to fix the phonetic tradition of the Hebrew Bible and serve as a reading guide. Nevertheless, different schools of vocalization and various traditions of Hebrew existed.[1]

Among these traditions, we find the Tiberian tradition, which prevailed over the others and is found in the Masoretic text, the Palestinian tradition and the Babylonian tradition, from the homonymous geographical areas. They produced vowels notation in the medieval period.

Other traditions, despite missing Masoretic vocalization, are nevertheless able to provide information about phonetic and morphological customs of the Hebrew language. These include the Samaritan tradition, i.e., the oral reading tradition of the Pentateuch in the Samaritan community recorded by Ben-Ḥayyim (2000), and the entire corpus of Qumran Hebrew. All of them reflect different Hebrew traditions. Each tradition fixes the pronunciation of Hebrew in a specific place and moment, that is, the century of its written stabilization. Therefore, the comparison between these traditions serves to reconstruct the history of the Hebrew language.

In this sense, the second column of Origen's *Hexapla*, the so called *Secunda*, which we refer to here as the Column, represents an autonomous tradition of Hebrew (Yuditsky 2017, 5).

As a phonetic transcription of Hebrew in the Greek alphabet (Mercati 1947, 4–5), the *Secunda* was mainly studied to provide insight into pronunciation of Hebrew before the Masoretic punctuation was fixed. Such an inquiry was carried out from two different points of view. First, the Greek consonantal graphemes represent a tool to verify the Hebrew pronunciation of consonants. Second, the presence of vocalic graphemes, required in Greek, was a tool by which to compare the Hebrew tradition of the *Secunda* to the other Hebrew traditions as far as phonetics and morphology are concerned. In this sense, the synoptic work of Origen's *Hexapla*, which was probably conceived as a philological edition of the Septuaginta based on the Greek versions of the Hebrew Bible (Kamesar 1993, 10), represented an important linguistic resource.

1 I would like to thank Prof. Corrado Martone and Prof. Steven E. Fassberg for their valuable suggestions. My deepest gratitude goes to Dr. Alexey E. Yuditsky for reading the text and providing precious remarks.

An important advancement in the studies on the *Secunda* was the edition of Frederick Field (1875), which collected both the hexaplaric fragments on the margin of manuscripts and the quotations from patristic literature. Therefore, his transcriptions are called 'external sources' (ES, henceforth). The quotations of Greek transcriptions of Hebrew words from the *Secunda* reported in the patristic literature seem to have been manipulated and adapted in time to the Greek language, as many samples reveal. However, the most relevant discovery in the study of the *Secunda* was the palimpsest fragment found by Giovanni Mercati (1958) in the Ambrosian Library in Milan. This additional text consists of thirteen fragments of different hexaplaric Psalms, not only from the *Secunda*, but also from other Greek versions of the Hebrew Bible. This discovery changes our knowledge of the *Secunda*. The Palimpsest fragments are not quotations from Origen's *Hexapla*, but an actual copy of all versions of the *Hexapla*, including the *Secunda*. Thus, the Greek transcriptions of the Hebrew words in the Palimpsest are to be considered authentic and comparable to other Hebrew traditions.

In the *Secunda*, the transcriptions are normally realized in accordance with the place and manner of articulation of the two languages, Greek and Hebrew.[2] In this respect, we distinguish three types of relationships between the Hebrew phonemes and the Greek graphemes:

1. Hebrew phonemes that have a perfect correspondence in Greek, for example, /m/ and /n/. In this example, both Hebrew and Greek graphemes, מ/μ and נ/ν, are the respective representation of the bilabial and alveolar nasal.
2. Hebrew phonemes that may share the place of articulation, but not the manner, with Greek phonemes. In this case, the transcriptions present an approximation in the use of the Greek graphemes, such as for voiceless palate-alveolar /š/ שׁ, for which the Greek had only the grapheme of the unvoiced sibilant σ as a valid correspondence. The approximation is, in this case, in the absence of sonority. Therefore, σ is the graphic representation of all voiceless sibilant fricatives, as also ס, צ and שׂ. Accordingly, the voiced sibilant fricative ז is represented by the Greek grapheme ζ.
3. Hebrew phonemes that completely lack a consonantal equivalent in Greek. This is the case in Hebrew (and in other Semitic languages) of the guttural consonants, both laryngeal (א, ה) and pharyngeal (ח, ע). These phonemes can be easily defined as Hebrew consonantal phonemes which

2 In this section, I deal only with the transcription criterion for a single phoneme; for a precise account about the pronunciation of the phonemes of the Column, see Kantor 2017, 182 ff.

are without a consonantal charge in Greek, in other words, they are not perceived as consonants by Greek speakers. This phenomenon is easily explained by the absence of these specific phonemes in other Indo-European languages (Lipínski 1997, 141). Thus, they are not directly represented (Kantor 2017, 226).

2 The Guttural Consonants in the *Secunda* Transcriptions

Because they tend to weaken and lose their consonantal sound, the guttural consonants have a particular status in Semitic languages (Mor 2013, 161). They represent a common problem not only in Greek transcriptions but also in Latin transcriptions. This problem is so severe that "with the exception of the quiescent Latin h, in certain positions, the glottals are never represented by a transcription sign" (Murtonen 1981, 68).[3]

In this regard, the *Secunda* makes no exception. The gutturals are not noted, but their presence in the original Hebrew words is detectable in the *Secunda*'s transcriptions by two indices: 1.) the presence of the only vowel in the transcription: עִקֵּשׁ /εκκης *Ps.* 18: 27, עַם /αμ *Ps.* 18: 28;[4] and 2.) the presence of a hiatus between two vowels, as in הָאֵל /αηλ *Ps.* 18: 31, or a vowel plus a digraph, as in תָּאִיר /θαειρ, *Ps.* 18: 29.

However, these are not the only two ways of recognizing an original guttural consonant in a Greek transcription. In the Greek transcriptions of the Septuaginta, for example, guttural consonants can be directly represented by a vowel sign, as the first α in חֶרְמוֹן/'Αερμών, Deut. 3: 8.[5] In two cases in the *Secunda*, an ι is used in correspondence with an initial guttural: הוֹשִׁיעָה /ιωσία *Ps.* 28: 9 and וְחַסְדִּי /ιεσ·δι *Ps.* 89: 34 (Yuditsky 2017, 31). Again, the gutturals mainly influence the original vocalism of the word toward the low vowel /a/.

3 Murtonen's 1981 vision and opinion of the notation of the laryngeals in Hieronymus' transcriptions was integrated by Brønno 1970.

4 This is an important sign of guttural presence in the original word because, in Biblical Hebrew, a syllable always begins with a consonant; Blau 1982, 70.

5 Krašovec 2010, 98 says that often "the letter (ה) is not expressed at all either in Greek or in Latin, or it is transcribed with a vowel." The representation of the guttural by the vowel is inferred by the present author from the mutual correspondence between the graphemes in the two languages. Myers 2020, 135, on the basis of the possible representation of the gutturals by the vowels as expressed by Krašovec 2010, affirms that "(…) not only the LXX provides more evidence for the pronunciation of gutturals than is often realized, but also that the direct representation of gutturals in 2 Esdras occurred much later than one might expect."

This influence also occurs in the Tiberian tradition, where the gutturals favor the *pataḥ*, which is homogeneous to them (Joüon and Muraoka 2011, 78–79). The fact that /a/ is the preferred quality for guttural consonants is also evident in the quality of the auxiliary *pataḥ furtivum* in the Masoretic text, enabling the pronounciation of final gutturals, but not consistently noted when the preceding sound is /ā/ (Mion 2008, 204). Furthermore, in the Samaritan tradition, where gutturals weaken to zero, the shift א<ע is sometimes blocked when *'ayin* is followed by an original a/å (Ben-Ḥayyim 2000, 41). Therefore, the presence of a low vowel favors the maintenance of the original guttural. The vowel change is also evident in some transcriptions of the second century C.E in papyri of the Judean desert: the name עגלה, biblical עֶגְלָה, is transcribed as ΕΓΛΑ in the Babatha archive (P. Yadin 1 12) but with initial A, as ΑΓΛΑ, in the Salome's archive (XḤev/Se 69).[6]

The *Secunda* provides evidence of the same process of assimilation of vowels to a low articulation in presence of an original guttural. This process is active in both verbal and nominal patterns (Yuditsky 2017, 88) because of its phonetic, non-morphological nature. Examples include the *qal* participle לֹחֲמָי /λωαμαϊ *Ps*. 35: 1; the prefixes of imperfect *hifil* אַצְמִיתֵם/ασμιθαυμ, *Ps*. 18: 41 and אַטֶּה/αττε, *Ps*. 49: 5; and perhaps the quality in the first vowel in the split of אֲהוֹדֶנּוּ /αωδεννου *Ps*. 28: 7. For the nominal patterns consider חֲנִית/ἀνίθ *Ps*. 46: 10 and עֲלוּמָיו/αλουμαυ *Ps*. 89: 46.

In most of these cases, a possible vowel lowering caused by original guttural is apparent because of the presence of the grapheme α when a different vowel is expected, on the basis of the specific משקל of the forms in the Column. In the participle, this is *qōtēl*, preserved for λωαμαϊ only in the first vowel (*λωεμαϊ); in the *hifʿil* imperfect, the original משקל is **yaqtil* (Joüon and Muraoka 2011, 148). This last משקל corresponds to the *Secunda yiqtīl*, expressed in the verbal conjugation by ε in the first syllable and ι in the second syllable.[7] Therefore, for αττε and ασμιθαυμ, speaking of a vowel lowering is imprecise. A more accurate description is the preservation of the original /a/ quality of **yaqtil*, because of the presence of a guttural. Furthermore, αωδεννου can be compared to תוֹצִיאֵנִי /θωωσιηνι *Ps*. 31: 5. When the split of a super-long vowel into two vowels takes place, the two resulting vowels do not necessarily show the same vocalic quality. So, the presence of /a/ in αωδεννου can depend on the presence of a guttural, based on the comparison with θοωσιηνι (Yuditsky 2017, 84).

6 See Lewis 1989; Cotton 1995; ead. 1997.

7 For the relationship between the original form **yaqtil* and the prefix *yiq-* in the *Secunda*, see Yuditsky 2017, 160.

Let us now look at the nouns. The comparison of חֲנִית/ἀνίθ *Ps.* 46: 10 and עֲלוּמָיו/αλουμαυ *Ps.* 89: 46 with the other forms present in the Column and belonging to the same משקל, respectively *qētelt* and *qetūl*, indicates that /a/ is probably the result of the influence of a guttural. However, different examples of vowel lowering exist. For example, in the following two cases, a vowel lowering could be active: The *qal* imperatives אֶהֱבוּ/αβου, *Ps.* 31: 24 and הֱיֵה /αϊη 31: 3. The interpretation of these cases, however, is uncertain. The reference pattern in the imperative can also be *qatal*, with /a/ as possibly the original vowel (Ben-Ḥayyim 2000, 183; Bauer and Laender 1922, 304) and not a lowering from *qitil*. The *qatal* משקל is attested for the imperative of the verb הי״י, in the Samaritan form היו/ayyu (Ben-Ḥayyim 1977, 81; id. 2000, 167).

In the suffixed infinitive בְּחָפְזִי /βααφζι, *Ps.* 31: 23 the /a/ can stand for the guttural. Nevertheless, the *qatl* משקל used to represent the *qal* infinitive forms with the added suffix is attested in the Palestinian tradition (Harviainen 1977, 161). Therefore, none of the cases listed above can exclude the existence of a parallel משקל, which is a morphological reason, opposite to the phonetic reason. And yet the presence of the guttural and the presence of /a/ is a remarkable coincidence in all the transcriptions.

The vowel lowering caused by gutturals is evident in other Hebrew traditions, apart from what is seen in the *Secunda*. In the Tiberian tradition, vowel lowering is particularly strong in the verbs with a guttural consonant in the radical set. In the Babylonian tradition, where the gutturals exhibit a distinction between ח, ה and ע, א (Yeivin 1985, 283–332), the פע״ע verbs present a *yiqtal* משקל along with the regularly employed *yiqtol* (Yeivin 1985, 464, 468). The Palestinian tradition has different tendencies for the verbs with a guttural radical, with *qameṣ* or *pataḥ* corresponding to the Tiberian *segol* (Harviainen 1977, 132). Furthermore, in the Palestinian tradition, there are some forms in which /e/ occurs in correspondence with the Tiberian *pataḥ*, as in the פ״אהחע verbs (Revell 1970, 64).

The cross-traditional comparison of vocalic patterns in the presence of a guttural can also be made in the case of the auxiliary vowel in segolate nouns. The Tiberian tradition often shows a vocalization in /a/ for על״אהחע nouns, as in נַחַל or סֶלַע (Joüon and Muraoka 2011, 223–224). The Palestinian tradition often presents an /e/ vowel in על״אהחע nouns of the non-Biblical texts, such as *meleḥ*, *neṣeḥ* (Harviainen 1977, 186–187; Yahalom 1997, 25), sometimes alternating with /a/ in the Biblical manuscripts (*melaḥ*; Yahalom 1969, 39). In the Babylonian tradition, the auxiliary vowel in segolate nouns is always *pataḥ*. In these contexts in the *Secunda* the vowel is generally /a/, for both ע״אהחע and ל״אהחע nouns. Consider שָׁחַת/σααθ Pss. 30: 10 and 49: 10; פַּחַד /φααδ *Ps.* 36: 2; וָבַעַר/ουβααρ *Ps.* 49: 11; פֶּשַׁע/φεσα *Ps.* 36: 2; יחד, in עָשִׁיר יַחַד/*ιααδ ασιρ and יַחַד/ιααδε *Ps.* 49: 3 and

11. There are only two exceptions with ε in two ל״ע nouns: בֶּצַע/ βεσε *Ps.* 30: 10, and רֶגַע/ρεγε *Ps.* 30: 6.

These examples demonstrate that the lowering of the vowel determined by guttural consonants is active in the tradition of the Column. The Column shares this phenomenon with various traditions of Hebrew, especially the Tiberian tradition, where the assimilation has a phonetic nature. Nevertheless, there are cases when a guttural consonant is concerned that the Greek transcriptions of the *Secunda* are different from other traditions. This difference is revealed by the preservation of the regular vocalization of the *qal* imperfect prefix for a פ״אהחע verb, against the assimilation in /a/, which is exhibited by the other traditions, and in some verbal forms of ע״חע. The analysis of these forms is the subject of the following section.

3 The Relationship between the Vowel and the Guttural in Some Verbal Forms of the *Secunda*

3.1 *The Vocalization of the Prefix in the* פ״אהחע *Verbs*

As shown above, some influence of guttural consonants on vocalism in the tradition of the *Secunda* is undeniable. Despite this influence, there are some verbal forms with a guttural where the lowering of the vowel is not frequently applied. These instances include the vocalization of the prefix of the imperfect verbs, as exhibited by almost all transcriptions. In the *qal* imperfect, the original *yaqtul* משקל of the active verbs always corresponds to the *yiqtol* in the *Secunda*, as in וְיַחְרְגוּ/ουϊερογου *Ps.* 18: 46 and אִם־יַעַזְבוּ/εμ·ϊεζεβοὺ *Ps.* 89: 31. The same correspondence is maintained with *yiqtal*, where /i/ could be the original vowel (Barth 1894): וְיַחְפְּרוּ/ουϊφρου *Ps.* 35: 26, יֶחְמְרוּ/ιέμρου *Ps.* 46: 4.[8] The two apparent exceptions are וַיַּעֲלֹז /ουαϊαλεζ *Ps.* 28: 7, belonging to the *yaqtil* משקל, and וְיַאֲמֵץ/ουιαεμας *Ps.* 31: 25. This last form, however, almost always belongs to *yiqtal* משקל in the different Hebrew traditions. Therefore, it is possibly a mistake, which should be corrected to *ουιεεμας (Yuditsky 2017, 123). The /a/ in ουαϊαλεζ is actually due to the guttural influence, and, as such, it remains the only case documented in the imperfect of first guttural verbs. Perhaps, according to the rarety of the *yaqtil* משקל, it can be a *hifil* imperfect, and not a *qal* (Yuditsky 2017, 123)?

8 The Barth-Ginsberg Law. Hasselbach 2005, 258: "the prefix vowel of the prefix or imperfect(ive) conjugation in the base [...] is dependent on the theme vowel of the respective verbal base. When the theme vowel is /i/ or /u/, the prefix vowel is /a/, while when the theme

We find the absence of assimilation to /a/ in the prefix vowel of imperfect verbs with first guttural radical in the next example from ES. In Mal. 2: 13, תַּעֲשׂוּ/θεσου occurs, and the prefix is vocalized with /e/ and not with /a/, as expected in ל״י verbs beginning with ע. This form is of great importance because it confirms the absence of /a/, even when the prefix is different from /y/, as in almost all the forms. Moreover, this transcription invalidates the hypothesis of the absence of /a/ due to assimilation /ya/>/yi/.[9]

In the *qal* imperfect, the form תֶּהְגֶּה/θαάγε *Ps.* 35: 28 invites some discussion. If θαάγε is actually an imperfect *qal*, as Brønno thinks (1943, 29), the first /a/ could be an actual evidence of the guttural influence. However, it is possible to suggest that the transcription represents the *pi*ʿʿ*el* θαγγε, corresponding to תְּהַגֶּה*. Mercati (1965, 163), accepted this possibility in light of the similarity of Α and Γ in oncial writing; and Yuditsky (2008, 238; 2017, 157) proved it, because of the presence of the auxiliary vowels exclusively with an /e/ sound. If the form is actually a *pi*ʿʿ*el*, /a/ is simply the vowel of the regular *yeqattel* משקל of the *pi*ʿʿ*el* imperfect, without any representation of the guttural; compare also וַתְּאַזְּרֵנִי/ουεθαζερηνι, *Ps.* 30: 12.

In the *nif*ʿ*al*, the picture is not so neat, because of the scarcity of the forms in the *Secunda*. The regular *niqtal* משקל of the perfect is always respected with strong and פ״א verbs (וְנֶאֶסְפוּ/*ουνεεσαφου *Ps.* 35: 15). The *naqtil* is found in the transcription וְנֶעֱזָרְתִּי /ου·νάζερθι *Ps.* 28: 7. The *naqtil* משקל is an isolate example of this phenomenon. The pharyngeal seems responsible for the vowel lowering, although Sperber (1937–1938, 246) proposes a correction in *νεζαρθι, supposing a switch in the regular vocalization α in the first syllable and ε in the second. Following paleographic considerations, Mercati (1965, 38) was convinced the transcription is correct, attributing the coloration /a/ to the influence of the guttural.

Regarding *pi*ʿʿ*el* forms, the /a/ in אֲחַלֵּל לֹא/λω·ααλλελ *Ps.* 89: 35 does not seem to depend on the guttural ח, because it is also found in other two verbs beginning with ש: אֲשַׁקֵּר /ασσακερ and אֲשַׁנֶּה/ασσανε, *Ps.* 89: 34 and 35.[10]

---

vowel is /a/, the prefix vowel is /i/." The law was first observed in Hebrew and Aramaic by Barth (1894); Ginsberg (1939, 318) found the same evidence in Ugaritic; Hasselbach 2005.

9 This is a frequent phonetic tendency in the *Secunda*: for the phenomenon /ya/>/yi/, we can only provide the form יְמִינוֹ/ιμινω *Ps.* 89: 26, belonging to the *qatīl* משקל which, however, presents the sole example of an initial grapheme ι in the transcription. For other nominal and verbal forms, see Yuditsky 2017, 96.

10 The transcriptions in question do not fit the *pi*ʿʿ*el* forms. In fact, they exhibit a redoubled first radical, as in the *nif*ʿ*al* imperfect (Yuditsky 2017, 152), and not in the second, as should

Not many פ״אהחע verbs are documented in the *Secunda.* The most significant are the *qal* imperfect forms. These forms correspond to the strong verbs belonging to the *yiqtol* משקל. Furthermore, where /i/ is expected because of the original *yiqtal,* the *Secunda* does not exhibit a tendency toward assimilation of /i/ to /a/, differently from what happens in the Tiberian forms that show the alternance יֶחְפַּר/יַחְפֹּר between *pataḥ* and *segol.* The ES confirm the tendency toward the generalization of the yi- prefix with the form תַּעֲשׂוּ/θεσου, vocalized with /e/. In order to shed light on this question, the comparison with other traditions can be enlightening, allowing us to understand the general behaviour of פ״אהחע verbs in the *qal* imperfect.

In the Tiberian tradition, the *yaqtul* משקל appears in active verbs and the *yiqtal* in the stative verbs. In the פ״א forms of stative verbs, the original /i/ and /a/ assimilate to the following laryngeal/pharyngeal, becoming a *segol* (Blau 1982, 238).[11] In the ל״י verbs, except for היה and חיה, the vowel of the prefix is *segol* before ה and ח and *pataḥ* before an initial ע. The Palestinian tradition exhibits a vocalization similar to the Tiberian tradition, with some exceptions in Biblical and mainly non-Biblical texts (Harviainen 1977, 183). Among these exceptions, the difference is found mostly in the Tiberian *pataḥ*/Palestinian *segol*, with only one exception. Palestinian /a/ corresponds to the Tiberian *segol* in תֶּאֱפוֹד/תאפוֹד (Harviainen 1977, 183). No difference for ל״י verbs exists.

In Samaritan Hebrew, the first ח prefers the /e/ vowel, but it sometimes alternates with /a/, regularly employed when ע is present (Ben-Ḥayyim 2000, 121); for example, in the contrast תחסם-*tēssåm*/תחדל-*tå:dål* and תעזב-*tåzzåb*, תעמד-*tåmmåd.*[12] The ל״י verbs normally have an /i-e/ vowel that becomes /a/ when the first radical is a guttural (Ben-Ḥayyim 2000, 162). However, the verb עש״י is vocalized with /e/ in all persons of the imperfect: תעשו-*tēššu* (Ben-Ḥayyim 2000, 168). The situation appears similar in the Babylonian tradition, where only א and ע are considered guttural consonants. The two others, ח and ה, are treated as strong consonants, having a regular vocalization with /i/ (Yeivin 1985, 287). Only the pharyngeal ח sometimes presents a *pataḥ* (Yeivin 1985, 455), as evident in the contrast between חמל belonging to *yaqtul* and חדל to *yiqtal* of the stative verbs (Yeivin 1985, 455, 457). Again, the פ״א verbs have *ṣere* in the ancient system (Yeivin 1985, 460) and פ״ע exhibit an /a/, with the variant of /i/, when they belong to the *yiqtal* משקל (Yeivin

---

be in the *piʿʿel* stem. However, they can be interpreted as *piʿʿel*, in which the reduplication, involving a first sibilant radical and a high vowel, as put by Kantor 2017, 243, "must be explained perceptually."

11 For additional details, Gumpertz 1953, 90–103.

12 For additional examples, Ben-Ḥayyim 2000, 121, 2.2.1.1.4 b.

1985, 461, 464). The ל״י verbs have in general a *ḥiriq* vocalization, also with gutturals.[13] Among these, עש״י and other initial ע are always vocalized with *pataḥ*.

In these cases, the different traditions exhibit an alternation between the two vowels /a/ and /i/ for the *qal* imperfect prefixes of the פ״אהחע verbs. The Tiberian tradition seems susceptible to the presence of the guttural and to the preservation of the original /a/ vowel (*pataḥ*), when a guttural follows (*yaqtul, yaqtil* against *yiqtal*); *pataḥ* is generally favored in the presence of *ʿayin*. The Palestinian tradition has more occurrences of the anterior vowel /e-i/ with respect to /a/. In the correspondence of three occurrences of *pataḥ* in the Tiberian punctuation, a *segol* appears in the Palestinian tradition, demonstrating a partial assimilation to the strong patterns (Harviainen 1977, 183). The opposition of Tiberian *pathaḥ* and Palestinian *segol* in the auxiliary vowel of the segolate nouns, as discussed section 2, demonstrates a similar trait. In the Babylonian and Samaritan traditions, the tendency toward /a/ is particularly strong when *ʿayin* is the first consonant of the root. The Samaritan tradition makes an exception only with the ל״י verb עש״י, where the prefix is vocalized with /e/.[14] The Babylonian tradition, on the contrary, seems to prefer /a/ in verbs with both ל״י and פ״ע. On the other hand, א is vocalized as /ē/, while ה and ח are not treated as gutturals in the Babylonian reading tradition, as evident from the entire language system.

To summarize, all traditions in the morphological context of the *qal* imperfect exhibit a mixed tendency between the assimilation of vowels to guttural consonants, and the preservation of the original vowel for guttural consonants, as evident in the use of /a/, and the progressive levelling and normalization according to the paradigm of the strong verbs, as illustrated by the anterior vowels /i-e/. This last is defined as *Systemzwang*, 'system coercion', which means pressure toward normalization exerted by strong verbs on the whole paradigm. Among the different traditions, the *Secunda* does not seem to disclose a definite tendency. Instead, the *Secunda* always uses the prefix /yi-/ of the strong verbs, i.e., of the *yiqtol* משקל, in all following cases: with original *yaqtul* for פ״אהחע verbs; with original *yiqtal*, in which there is never tendency to assimilation; and with the verb עש״י, as is evident from the ES. The only exception is found in the

13 For the initial *ʾaleph*, we only have the root את״י, presenting *sewa'* at the beginning; Yeivin 1985, 701.

14 In the Samaritan tradition, in the form with an /e/ in the prefix, the original vowel is /i/, not /ē/. The presence of the long vowel in this context is due to the stress and, as a result, to the alternation of i/ē; Ben-Ḥayyim 2000, 76.

yaqtil משקל of ουαϊαλεζ. Nevertheless, the rarity of this kind of משקל could suggest an occasional assimilation of the vowel to the *ʿayin*, by thus excluding the real preservation of /a/ in the prefix before a guttural consonant.[15]

It is difficult to investigate the tendency to the assimilation of vowels to gutturals for the *nifʿal* stem because not as many examples are available in the *Secunda*. The original משקל for the participle and the perfect is *naqtal*, later becoming *niqtal* (Qimron and Sivan 1995–1996, 19 ff.). In the Tiberian tradition, the regular prefix is *segol*. *Pataḥ* occurs rarely, only in the infinitive absolute, for example: נַעֲמוֹד (Joüon and Muraoka 2011, 167). In comparison, the Palestinian tradition presents forms with *segol* and with /i/, indicating the progressive assimilation to the strong pattern, as it happens in the *qal* (Harviainen 1977, 180). Nevertheless, as regards the Palestinian *qal* imperfect, in which one example had q/a/ corresponding to the Tiberian *segol* (Harviainen 1977, 183), the process of normalization is more complete in the *nifʿal*: Among the 12 occurrences with verbs with first pharyngeal consonant root, 5 are with *ḥiriq*.

The traditions other than Palestinian also exhibit a progressive replacement of /a/ with the /i/ in the strong verb, according to the *Systemzwang*. In the Babylonian tradition, for the פ״ע , פ״א and ל״י verbs, the /e/ or /a/ vowels of the ancient system proceed toward e/i in the non-Biblical texts of the medial stage, with a total replacement with /i/ in the late system (Yeivin 1985, 501–502). Thus, in the Babylonian tradition, this process is chronological. The Samaritan tradition presents minor differences between the perfect and the participle stems. The regular /i/ is found in the perfect, like in נערמו-*niyyårāmu* or נאסף-*niyyåsåf*; partial exceptions only occur in verbs without gemination in the first radical (ונעלמה-*wnå:låmå*, ונאכל-*wnåkkel*; Ben-Ḥayyim 2000, 125). In the Samaritan participle, /a/ appears in correspondence to the Tiberian *segol*: ונאמן-*wnå:mən*, ונאמנים-*wnå:mēnəm* (Ben-Ḥayyim 2000, 193).

The *Secunda*, as already said, has a few occurrences of the *nifʿal* stem for פ״אהחע verbs: just the perfects וְנֶאֶסְפוּ/*ουνεεσαφου *Ps*. 35: 15 and וְנֶעֱזָרְתִּי/ου·νάζερθι *Ps*. 28: 7 and the participles נֶאֱמָן/νεεμαν and נֶאֱמֶנֶת/νεεμάναθ *Ps*. 89: 38 and 29. The presence of the expected *niqtal* in the אמן and אסף verbs contrasts with the actual *naqtil* of νάζερθι. In this case, the *naq-* of the משקל in question is probably a result of the preservation of /a/ because of the presence of *ʿayin*.[16] Therefore, because of the absence of more forms in the *Secunda*, where /a/

15 This would be perfectly coherent with the phonetic phenomenon of assimilation, which results because of the "speaker's inertia, endeavoring to speak with the least possible effort," according to Blau 1982, 57.

16 The presence of ε is probably caused by the influence of the sonore sibilant ζ or by a dissimilation; Yuditsky 2017, 94 and 147.

would not be expected according to the other traditions, we do not have enough data for comparison and we cannot say in confidence if the *naq-* prefix was preserved or was the outcome of an occasional assimilation, as it is in ουαϊαλεζ. Notably, in the *Secunda*, the only two cases with /a/ prefix are in verbs פ״ע; the pharyngeal consonant may have still been perceived in this position at the time of the redaction of the Column.

3.2 *Some Forms of* ע״חע *Verbs*

As seen in 3.1, at least for the *qal* imperfect in פ״אהחע verbs the various traditions exhibit a progressive *Systemzwang* toward /i/ from /a/ and a mixed employment of /a/ and /i/. This progression is the result of a tendency of coercion of the strong paradigms verbs of the preservation of the original /a/ vowel for the guttural consonants and the phonetic assimilation of vowels to the guttural—a phonetic phenomenon that makes /a/ part of the morphological reference pattern.

In this regard, the *Secunda* does not show the /a/ vowel in the prefix of *yiqtol*, which appears as yi-. The presence of yi- in *yiqtol* forms of verbs with first guttural root consonant shows a contradictory tendency as regards the assimilation of vowels to guttural consonants, a phenomenon which is well attested in other forms in the *Secunda*. Thus, the *Secunda* shows the tendency to extend the משקל of the strong verbs to all verbal forms. The only exception is in a פ״ע verb exhibiting the rare *yaqtil* משקל. Indeed, with the *ʿayin* consonant the assimilation occurs also in the *nifʿal*.

The absence of assimilation of vowels to gutturals, in contexts in which assimilation is expected and present in other traditions of Hebrew, is revealed in the *Secunda* also in some occurrences of ע״ח verbs: אֶמְחָצֵם/εμωσημ, וְאֶשְׁחָקֵם/ οὐεσοκημ, in *Ps.* 18, 39 and 43, and perhaps also תִסְעָדֵנִי/*θεσοδηνι, *Ps.* 18: 36.[17] In the Tiberian tradition, the forms אֶמְחָצֵם /εμωσημ, וְאֶשְׁחָקֵם /οὐεσοκημ, in *Ps.* 18, 39 and 43, and תִסְעָדֵנִי /*θεσοδηνι, *Ps.* 18, 36 all belong to the *yiqtal* משקל in Tiberian Hebrew, precisely because of the presence of a guttural as the second radical (Joüon and Muraoka 2011, 79, 169). The *qameṣ* in the Masoretic text depends on the pre-tonic lengthening of /a/ in open pre-tonic syllables, as in ל״אהחע verbs; e.g., יִשְׁמָעֵנִי compared to יִשְׁמְרֵנִי. Moreover, in the Babylonian system, the two forms εμωσημ and οὐεσοκημ are documented in the *yiqtal* משקל (Yeivin 1985, 471). These last examples are essential because they prove that in the Babylonian tradition the regular pattern is *yiqtal*.

17 The original form of the Palimpsest, θεσ*δηνι, can be corrected by the insertion of *omicron* between σ and δ, probably blurred in the manuscript; Mercati 1965, 13; Yuditsky 2017, 118.

In the same context in which the Tiberian tradition exhibits a pre-tonic lengthening of /a/, the Babylonian pre-tonic /o/ is also preserved and lengthened (Blau 1982, 224; Yeivin 1985, 469–470). The three forms transcribed in the Column (אֶמְחָצֵם /εμωσημ, וְאֶשְׁחָקֵם /οὐεσοχημ, *Ps.* 18, 39 and 43, and תִּסְעָדֵנִי /*θεσοδηνι, *Ps.* 18, 36) show the presence of a pharyngeal as the second consonant of the root, ע or ח; they belong to the משקל of strong verbs, i.e., *yiqtol*.

The vowel of the second radical consonant of the *qal* imperfect is related to the vowel in the same position in the imperative. Regarding verbs ע״חע, this relationship is evident in the Tiberian tradition. In ע״אהחע verbs, the imperfect generalizes the /a/ (typical of the stative verbs), because of the tendency to substitute the original vowel, /u/ or /i/, with *pataḥ* in a stressed closed syllable (Joüon and Muraoka 2011, 79, 169), again because of the influence of guttural consonants on vowels.

In addition, in the Samaritan tradition the relationship between the imperfect and the imperative is strong. The vowel of the second root consonant for ע״אהחע verbs is the same as that of the imperfect, that is, /a/ of the *yiqtal* משקל (Ben-Ḥayyim 2000, 183–184). Compare the verb בחר, *yēʾbār* in the imperfect and *bār* in the imperative (Ben-Ḥayyim 1977, 51; 2000, 128).

In the Babylonian tradition these verbs generally present a *pataḥ* vocalization in the stem, which may alternate with *ḥolem*, when the second radical consonant is pharyngeal. This is mainly true for non-Biblical manuscripts (Yeivin 1985, 485). The Tiberian tradition generally shows *pataḥ*. Interestingly, in some cases, Tiberian *pataḥ* corresponds to Babylonian *ḥolem* in the same word. The imperative לְחַם of the Masoretic text corresponds to Babylonian לחֹם (Yeivin 1985, 485).

In the imperative of verbs with a guttural consonant as the second radical, the *Secunda* does not seem to show any assimilation caused by guttural consonants. The form λοομ *Ps.* 35: 1 probably belongs to the original *qutul* משקל (Bauer and Leander 1922, 304), as does זְכֹר/ηζχορ, *Ps.* 89: 51.[18] The presence of the pharyngeal as the second radical consonant does not prime vowel lowering. In the *Secunda*, λοομ represents the only case for the *qal* imperative of any ע״אהחע verb. With lack of additional data, we cannot completely exclude that the second /o/ in λοομ is due to a phonetic reason, i.e., the assimilation of the vowel to the final labial consonant μ.

18 It is interesting that the same form, *zēkor*, is preserved in Samaritan Hebrew, where short /u/ normally is not allowed; the validity of this interpretation is confirmed by the plural forms *šēmåru* and *zēkåru*, which are to be regarded as remnants of the infinitive absolute form; Ben-Ḥayyim 1977, 87; id. 2000, 184.

The assimilation of vowels to labial consonants is attested elsewhere in the Column, for example in the *pi*ʿʿ*el* participle מְשַׁוֶּה/μοσαυε *Ps.* 18: 34. Nonetheless, a noteworthy morphological parallel is found in the Babylonian tradition: the *qtol* משקל is present specifically with the verb לחֹם, לחם, and in general with ע״חע verbs (e.g., רחֹץ; Yeivin 1985, 485). Thus, the preservation of the original vowel /u/ in the *Secunda* seems plausible, despite the presence of a guttural as the second radical consonant.

In the imperfective stem vowel of the ע״חע verbs, the *Secunda* again does not seem to apply any assimilation to the guttural articulation. This kind of assimilation is responsible for transforming *yiqtol* into *yiqtal* משקל in the Tiberian and the Babylonian traditions. In both traditions, a phonetic phenomenon (assimilation to guttural articulation) generalizes the /a/, rendering it morphological in the paradigm (*yiqtal* משקל).

4 Conclusions

In a number of forms where other Hebrew traditions show the generalization of a משקל caused by the influence of guttural consonants on vowels, the *Secunda* has the tendency to maintain the pattern of the strong verbs, i.e., not to assimilate vowels to the guttural consonants. This tendency is mainly evident from the prefix yi- instead of ya- in the *qal* imperfect of פ״אהחע verbs, and in some forms with pharyngeal consonants as second radical consonants in the *qal* imperfect and imperative. This happens despite the pervasive influence of gutturals on vowels in the Column. The tendency of the Column to generalize patterns of strong verbs to guttural verbs can be proved by the comparison with other traditions of Hebrew, where we can easily track the result of opposite forces. These forces are: The preservation of the original /a/ because of the guttural; the assimilation of the gutturals toward the low vowel /a/; and the *Systemzwang* toward normalization of the patterns of non-strong verbs, according to the patterns of strong verbs.

References

Barth, Jacob. 1894. "Zur vergleichenden semitischen Grammatik." *ZDMG* 48: 1–21.

Bauer Hans, and Leander, Pontus. 1922. *Historische Grammatik der hebräischen Sprache des Alten Testamentes*. Tübingen Halle (Saale): Max Niemeyer.

Ben-Ḥayyim, Ze'ev. 1977. *The Literary and Oral Tradition of Hebrew and Aramaic amongst the Samaritans*. Vol 4, *The Words of the Pentateuch* (Hebrew). Jerusalem: The Academy of the Hebrew Language.

Ben-Ḥayyim, Ze'ev. 2000. *A Grammar of Samaritan Hebrew: Based on the Recitation of the Law and Comparison with the Tiberian and Other Jewish tradition*. Revised in English by Ze'ev Ben-Ḥayyim and Abraham Tal. Jerusalem—Winona Lake, Ind.: The Hebrew University Magnes Press—Eisenbrauns.

Blau, Joshua. 1982. *Phonology and Morphology of Biblical Hebrew*. Winona Lake, Ind.: Eisenbrauns.

Brønno, Einar. 1943. *Studien über hebräische Morphologie und Vokalismus auf Grundlage der mercatischen Fragmente der zweiten Kolumne der Hexapla des Origenes*. Leipzig: Brockhaus.

Brønno, Einar. 1970. *Die Aussprache der hebräischen Laryngale nach Zeugnissen des Hieronymus*. Aarhus: Universitetsforlaget.

Cotton, Hannah M. 1995. "*The Archive of Salome Komaise Daughter of Levi: Another Archive from the 'Cave of letters'*." *Zeitschrift für Papyrologie und Epigraphik* 105: 171–208.

Cotton, Hannah M., and Yardeni, Ada. 1997. *Aramaic, Hebrew and Greek Documentary Texts from Naḥal Ḥever and Other Sites*. Discoveries in the Judean Desert XVII. Oxford: Clarendon.

Dotan, Aron. 1981. "The Relative Chronology of Hebrew Vocalization and Accentuation." *Proceedings of the American Academy for Jewish Research* 48: 87–99.

Field, Frederick. 1875. *Origen Hexapla*. Oxford: Clarendon.

Ginsberg, H. Louis. 1939. "Two Religious Borrowings in Ugaritic Literature." *Orientalia* 8: 317–327.

Gumpertz, Yehiel (Gedalyahu). 1953. *Mivṭa'e śefatenu: Studies in Historical Phonetics of the Hebrew* Language. (Hebrew). Jerusalem: Mosad Harav Kook.

Harviainen, Tapani. 1977. *On the Vocalism of the Closed Unstressed Syllables in Hebrew*. Studia Orientalia 48:1. Helsinki: The Finnish Oriental Society.

Hasselbach, Rebecca. 2005. "Barth-Ginsberg Law." In *Encyclopedia of Hebrew Language and Linguistics*, vol 1, edited by Geoffrey Kahn et al., 258–259, Leiden—Boston: Brill.

Joüon, Paul, and Muraoka, Takamitsu. 2011. *A Grammar of Biblical Hebrew*. 3rd reprint of 2nd ed. Rome: Gregorian & Biblical Press.

Kamesar, Adam. 1993. *Jerome, Greek Scholarship, and the Hebrew Bible—A Study of the Quaestiones Hebraicae in Genesis*. Oxford: Clarendon.

Kantor, Benjamin Paul. 2017. "The Second Column of Origen's *Hexapla* in the Light of Greek Pronunciation." PhD diss., University of Texas at Austin.

Krašovec, Jože. 2010. *The Transformation of Biblical Proper Names*. London: T&T Clark.

Lewis, Napthali. 1989. *The Documents from the Bar-Kokhba Period in the Cave of Letters—Greek Papyri*. Jerusalem: The Hebrew University of Jerusalem.

Lipínski, Edward. 1997. *Semitic Languages: Outline of Comparative Grammar*. OLA 80. Leuven: Peeters.

Mercati, Giovanni. 1947. "Il problema della II colonna dell'Esaplo." *Biblica* 28: 1–30.

Mercati, Giovanni. 1958. *Psalterii Hexapli Reliquiae. Pars Prima: Codex rescriptus Bybliothecae Ambrosianae O 39 sup. phototypice expressus et transcriptus*. Rome: Bibliotheca Vaticana.

Mercati, Giovanni. 1965. *Psalterii Hexapli reliquaie. Pars Prima: "Osservazioni". Commento critico al testo dei frammenti esaplari*. Rome: Bibliotheca Vaticana.

Mion, Giuliano. 2008. "Le pataḥ furtivum en sémitique. Rémarques de phonétique et phonologie." *VIII Afro-Asiatic Congress*. Studi Magrebini 6. Edited by Sergio Baldi, 203–212. Naples: Università degli Studi di Napoli "L'Orientale".

Mor, Uri. 2013. "Guttural Consonants: Pre-Masoretic". In *Encyclopedia of Hebrew Language and Linguistics*, vol 2, edited by Geoffrey Kahn et al., 161–165, Leiden—Boston: Brill.

Murtonen, Aimo. 1981. "Methodological Preliminaries to a Study of Greek (and Latin) Transcriptions of Hebrew." *Abr-Nahrain* 20: 60–73.

Myers, Pete. 2020. "The Representation of Gutturals by Vowels in the LXX of 2 Esdras." In *Studies in Semitic Vocalisation and Reading Traditions*, edited by Aaron D. Hornkohl and Geoffrey Kahn, 133–145, Cambridge: Open Book Publishers.

Qimron, Elisha and Sivan, Daniel. 1995–1996. "Interchanges of Pataḥ and Ḥiriq and the Attenuation Law." (Hebrew). *Lešonenu* 59: 7–38.

Revell, Ernest J. 1970. "Studies in Palestinian Vocalization of Hebrew." In *Essays on the Ancient Semitic World*, edited by John W. Wevers and Donald B. Redford, 59–100. Toronto: University of Toronto.

Sperber, Alexander. 1937–1938. "Hebrew Based upon Greek and Latin Transliterations." *Hebrew Union College Annual* 12–13: 103–274.

Yahalom, Joseph. 1969. "The Palestinian Vocalization in Hedwata's Qedustot, and the Language Tradition it Reflects." (Hebrew). *Lešonenu* 34: 25–60.

Yahalom, Joseph. 1997. *Palestinian Vocalised Piyyut Manuscripts in the Cambridge Genizah Collections*. Cambridge University Library Genizah Series 7. Cambridge: Cambridge University.

Yeivin, Israel. 1985. *The Hebrew Language Tradition as Reflected in the Babylonian Vocalization*. (Hebrew). Jerusalem: The Academy of the Hebrew Language.

Yuditsky, Alexey (Eliyahu). 2008. "The Weak Consonants in the Language of the Dead Sea Scrolls and in the *Hexapla* Transliteration." In *Conservatism and Innovation in the Hebrew Language of the Hellenistic Period*. Proceedings of a Fourth International Symposium on the Hebrew of the Dead Sea Scrolls & Ben Sira, edited by Jan Joosten and Jean-Sébastian Rey, 233–239. Leiden—Boston: Brill.

Yuditsky, Alexey (Eliyahu). 2017. *A Grammar of the Hebrew of Origen's Transcriptions*. (Hebrew). Jerusalem: The Academy of the Hebrew Language.